Quick Solutions to
Common
Errors
in
English

Quick Solutions to
Common
Errors
in
English

Angela Burt

An A-Z guide

to spelling,

punctuation

and grammar

howtobooks

Published by How To Books Ltd, 3 Newtec Place,
Magdalen Road, Oxford OX4 1RE. United Kingdom.
Tel: (01865) 793806. Fax: (01865) 248780.
email: info@howtobooks.co.uk
www.howtobooks.co.uk

First edition 2000
Second edition 2002
Third edition 2004
Reprinted 2004

British Library Cataloguing in Publication Data
A catalogue record for this book is available from the British Library.

Cover Design by Baseline Arts, Oxford
Produced for How To Books by Deer Park Productions, Tavistock
Typeset by PDQ Typesetting, Stoke-on-Trent, Staffs.
Printed and bound by Bell & Bain Ltd, Glasgow

NOTE: The material contained in this book is set out in good faith
for general guidance and no liability can be accepted
for loss or expense incurred as a result of relying in particular
circumstances on statements made in the book. Laws and regulations
are complex and liable to change, and readers should check the
current position with the relevant authorities before making
personal arrangements.

Quick Solutions to Common Errors in English is a reference book which has been written for the student and the general reader. It aims to tackle the basic questions about spelling, punctuation, grammar and word usage that the student and the general reader are likely to ask.

Throughout the book there are clear explanations, and exemplar sentences where they are needed. When it's helpful to draw attention to spelling rules and patterns, these are given so that the reader is further empowered to deal with hundreds of related words. The aim always has been to make the reader more confident and increasingly self-reliant.

This is a fast-track reference book. It is not a dictionary although, like a dictionary, it is arranged alphabetically. It concentrates on problem areas; it anticipates difficulties; it invites cross-references. By exploring punctuation, for example, and paragraphing, it goes far beyond a dictionary's terms of reference. It is not intended to replace a dictionary; it rather supplements it.

Once, in an evening class, one of my adult students said, 'If there's a right way to spell a word, I want to know it.' On another occasion, at the end of a punctuation session on possessive apostrophes, a college student said rather angrily, 'Why wasn't I told this years ago?'

This book has been written to answer all the questions that my students over the years have needed to ask. I hope all who now use it will have their questions answered also and enjoy the confidence and the mastery that this will bring.

Angela Burt

How to use this book

For ease of reference, all the entries in this book have been listed alphabetically rather than being divided into separate spelling, usage, punctuation and grammar sections.

You will therefore find **hypocrisy** following **hyphens**; **paragraphing** following **paraffin**; **who or whom?** following **whiskey or whisky?**; and so on.

Want to check a spelling?

Cross-referencing will help you locate words with tricky initial letters.

aquaint	Wrong spelling. See ACQUAINT.

Plural words are given alongside singular nouns, with cross-referencing to relevant rules and patterns.

knife (singular)	knives (plural). See PLURALS (v).

There is also a general section on **plurals** and another on **foreign plurals**.

If it's the complication of adding an ending that is causing you trouble, you will find some words listed with a useful cross-reference.

---

dining or dinning?
  dine + ing = dining (as in dining room)
  din + ing = dinning (noise dinning in ears)
  See ADDING ENDINGS (i) and (ii).

There are individual entries for confusing endings like
-able/-ible; **-ance,-ant/-ence,-ent**; **-cal/-cle**; **-ise or**
-ize? and for confusing beginnings like **ante-/anti-**; **for-/**
fore-; **hyper-/hypo-**; **inter-/intra-** and many others.

Usage?

If you're hesitating between two words in a tricky pair
(like **contagious or infectious?**; **disinterested or**
uninterested?; **imply or infer?**; **irony or sarcasm?**),
turn to whichever word is listed first alphabetically.
There you will find a full explanation of the difference
in meaning and usage. There will be a cross-reference
from the word listed second alphabetically.

---

misplace   See DISPLACE OR MISPLACE?.

Punctuation?

The functions of the different punctuation marks are
discussed under individual entries; **apostrophes** (');
brackets (round and square); **capital letters**; **colons** (:);
dashes (–); **exclamation marks** (!); **full stops** (.);
hyphens (-); **inverted commas/quotation marks/**
speech marks (single ' ' and double " "); **semicolons** (;);
and question marks (?).
   Additional entries include **commands**; **contractions**;
end stops; and **indirect/reported speech**.
   As well as the general entry, **contractions**,
commonly used contractions are listed individually as
the punctuation of these causes so much confusion.

---

isn't
   Place the apostrophe carefully. (*not* is'nt)

Grammar?

Many grammatical queries can be listed individually or as a choice between two or three possibilities. Among these are: **as or like?**; **consist in or consist of?**; **different from/to/than**; **due to or owing to?**; **fewer or less?**; **I/me/myself**; **lay or lie?**; **passed or past?**; **shall or will?**; **should or would?**; **who or whom?**.

---

between you and I
    Incorrect.
    Write: between you and me.
    See PREPOSITIONS.

theirselves
    Incorrect formation.
    See THEMSELVES.

At other times, however, some grammatical points have necessarily to be grouped under general technical headings which sound rather forbidding. (The entries themselves, I hope, will make all clear!)

These entries are too long to be quoted here. I suggest that you look them up to see whether they deal with areas that cause you problems:

> **comparative and superlative**
> **double negatives**
> **nouns**
> **paragraphing**
> **participles**
> **possessive pronouns**
> **prepositions**
> **sequence of tenses**
> **split infinitives**
> **subjunctive**

As well as using this book as a reference text (its unwritten subtitle is *A Friend at Your Elbow*!), I hope you will sometimes be tempted to browse and to follow up cross-references. Our language is a fascinating one and well repays careful attention.

There will come a time when you no longer need the guidance this reference book offers. That will be real success!

Appendices

At the end of the book there are three appendices for further reference:

Appendix A: Literary terms
Appendix B: Parts of speech
Appendix C: Planning, drafting and proofreading

abandon
  abandoned, abandoning, abandonment (*not* -bb-)

abattoir
  (*not* -bb-)

abbreviate
  abbreviated, abbreviating, abbreviation (*not* -b-)

abbreviations
  See CONTRACTIONS.

-able/-ible
  Adjectives ending in -able or -ible can be difficult to spell because both endings sound identical. You'll always need to be on guard with these words and check each word individually when you are in doubt, but here are some useful guidelines:

  (i) Generally use -able when the companion word ends in -ation:

      abominable, abomination
      irritable, irritation

  (ii) Generally use -ible when the companion word ends in -ion:

      comprehensible, comprehension
      digestible, digestion

  (iii) Use -able after hard c and hard g:

      practicable (c sounds like k)
      navigable (hard g)

  (iv) Use -ible after soft c and soft g:

      forcible (c sounds like s)
      legible (g sounds like j)

  See also ADDING ENDINGS (ii); SOFT C AND SOFT G.

abridgement/abridgment
Both spellings are correct. Use either but be consistent within one piece of writing.

abscess
This is a favourite word in spelling quizzes. (*not* absess or abcess)

absence
absent (*not* absc-)

absolute
absolutely (*not* absoloute, absoloutely)

absorb
absorption. Notice how b changes to p here.

abstract nouns
See NOUNS.

accept or except?
We **ACCEPT** your apology.
Everybody was there **EXCEPT** Stephen.

accessary or accessory?
If you want to preserve the traditional distinction in meaning between these two words, use **ACCESSARY** to refer to someone associated with a crime and **ACCESSORY** to refer to something that is added (a fashion accessory or car accessories). However, the distinction has now become blurred and it is perfectly acceptable to use one spelling to cover both meanings. Of the two, accessory is the more widely used, but both are correct.

accessible
(*not* -able)

accidentally
The adverb is formed by adding -ly to accidental. (*not* accidently)

accommodation
This is a favourite word in spelling quizzes and is frequently seen misspelt on painted signs.
(*not* accomodation or accommadation)

accross
Wrong spelling. See ACROSS.

accumulate
(*not* -mm-)

achieve
achieved, achieving, achievement (*not* -ei-) See also
ADDING ENDINGS (ii.); EI/IE SPELLING RULE.

acknowledgement/acknowledgment
Both spellings are correct but be consistent within one piece of writing.

acquaint
acquainted (*not* aq-)

acquaintance
(*not* -ence)

acquiesce
acquiesced, acquiescing (*not* aq-)

acquiescence
(*not* -ance)

acquire
acquired, acquiring, acquisition (*not* aq-)

acreage
Note that there are three syllables here. (*not* acrage)

across
(*not* accross)

adapter or adaptor?
Traditional usage would distinguish between these two words and reserve -er for the person (an adapter

→

of novels, for instance) and -or for the piece of electrical equipment. However, the distinction has become very blurred and the two spellings are considered by many authorities to be interchangeable. Use either for both meanings but be consistent within a single piece of writing.

addendum (singular) addenda (plural)
See FOREIGN PLURALS.

adding endings
Usually endings (suffixes) can be added to base words without any complications. You just add them and that is that!

e.g. iron + ing   = ironing
     steam + er   = steamer
     list + less   = listless

However, there are four groups of words which need especial care. Fortunately, there are some straightforward rules which save your learning thousands of words individually.

(i)   *The 1-1-1 rule*
     This rule applies to:
     words of   ONE syllable
     ending with   ONE consonant
     preceded by   ONE vowel.
     e.g. drop, flat, sun, win

When you add an ending beginning with a consonant to a l-l-l word, there is no change to the base word:

drop + let   = droplet
flat + ly   = flatly
win + some   = winsome
See CONSONANTS.

When you add an ending beginning with a vowel to a l-l-l word, you double the final letter of the base word:

```
drop + ed        = dropped
flat + est       = flattest
win + ing        = winning
sun + *y         = sunny
```
*y counts as a vowel when it sounds like i or e.
See VOWELS.

Treat qu as one letter:

```
quit + ing       = quitting
quip + ed        = quipped
```

Don't double final w and x. They would look
very odd and so we have correctly:

```
tax + ing        = taxing
paw + ed         = pawed
```

(ii) *The magic -e rule*
This rule applies to all words ending with a
silent -e.
e.g. hope, care, achieve, sincere, separate

When you add an ending beginning with a
consonant, keep the -e:

```
hope + ful       = hopeful
care + less      = careless
sincere + ly     = sincerely
separate + ly    = separately
achieve + ment   = achievement
```

When you add an ending beginning with a
vowel, drop the -e:

```
hope + ing       = hoping
care + er        = carer
sincere + ity    = sincerity
separate + ion   = separation
achieve + ed     = achieved
```

Do, however, keep the -e in words like singeing
(different from singing) and dyeing (different

→

from dying) and whenever you need to keep the identity of the base word clear (e.g. shoeing, canoeing).

Do remember to keep the -e with soft c and soft g words. It's the e that keeps them soft (courageous, traceable). (See SOFT C AND SOFT G.)

Don't keep the -e with these eight exceptions to the rule: truly, duly, ninth, argument, wholly, awful, whilst, wisdom.

(iii) *-y rule*

This rule applies to all words ending in -y. Look at the letter before the -y in the base word.

It doesn't matter at all what kind of ending you are adding. When you add an ending to a word ending in a vowel + y, keep the y:

portray + ed   = portrayed
employ + ment   = employment

When you add an ending to a word ending in a consonant + y, change the y to i:

try + al   = trial
empty + er   = emptier
pity + less   = pitiless
lazy + ness   = laziness

Do keep the y when adding -ing. Two i's together would look very odd, despite our two words ski-ing and taxi-ing.

try + ing   = trying
empty + ing   = emptying

Don't apply the rule in these fourteen cases: daily, gaily, gaiety, laid, paid, said, slain, babyhood, shyly, shyness, dryness, slyness, wryly, wryness.

(iv) *The 2-1-1 rule*

This rule applies to:

words of	TWO syllables
ending with	ONE consonant
preceded by	ONE vowel.

With this rule, it all depends on which syllable of the word is stressed. The 2-1-1 words below are stressed on the first syllable, and both vowel and consonant endings are added without any complications:

gossip	gossiping
target	targeted
limit	limitless
eager	eagerness

But note that kidnap, outfit, worship, always double their final letter:

kidnapped, outfitter, worshipping

Take care with 2-1-1 words which are stressed on the second syllable. There is no change when you add a consonant ending:

| forget + ful | = forgetful |
| equip + ment | = equipment |

Double the final consonant of the base word when you add a vowel ending:

forget + ing	= forgetting
equip + ed	= equipped
forbid + en	= forbidden
begin + er	= beginner

This rule is really valuable but you must be aware of some exceptions:

◆ 2-1-1 words ending in -l seem to have a rule all of their own. Whether the stress is on the first or the second syllable, there is no change when →

a consonant ending is added:

quarrel + some   = quarrelsome
instal + ment   = instalment

Double the -l when adding a vowel ending:

quarrel + ing   = quarrelling
instal + ed   = installed
excel + ent   = excellent

◆   Notice how the change of stress in these words
    affects the spelling:

confer	conferred	conferring	conference
defer	deferred	deferring	deference
infer	inferred	inferring	inference
prefer	preferred	preferring	preference
refer	referred	referring	reference
transfer	transferred	transferring	transference

See also -ABLE/-IBLE; -ANCE,-ANT/-ENCE,-ENT; -CAL/-CLE;
-FUL;-LY.

address
(*not* adr-)

adieu (singular) adieus or adieux (plural)
See FOREIGN PLURALS.

adrenalin/adrenaline
Both spellings are correct.

adress
Wrong spelling. See ADDRESS.

advantageous
advantage + ous
Keep the -e in this instance.
See SOFT C AND SOFT G.

adverse or averse?
These two words have different meanings.

The ferries were cancelled owing to **ADVERSE** weather conditions. (= unfavourable)
She is not **AVERSE** to publicity. (= opposed)

advertisement

advertise + ment
See ADDING ENDINGS (ii).

advice or advise?

My **ADVICE** is to forget all about it. (noun = recommendation)
What would you **ADVISE** me to do? (verb = recommend)

adviser or advisor?

Adviser is the traditionally correct British spelling. Advisor is more common in American English.

advisory

(*not* -ery)

aerial

Use the same spelling for the noun (a television **AERIAL**) and the adjective (an **AERIAL** photograph).

affect or effect?

Use these exemplar sentences as a guide:

Heavy drinking will **AFFECT** your liver. (verb)
The **EFFECT** on her health was immediate. (noun)
The new manager plans to **EFFECT** sweeping changes. (verb = to bring about)

afraid

(*not* affraid)

ageing or aging?

Both spellings are correct but many would prefer ageing as it keeps the identity of the base word (age) more easily recognised.
See ADDING ENDINGS (ii).

aggravate

Strictly speaking, aggravate means to make worse.

His rudeness **AGGRAVATED** an already explosive situation.

It is, however, widely used in the sense of to irritate or to annoy. Be aware that some authorities would regard this second usage as incorrect.

aggressive

(*not* agr-)

agree to/agree with

The choice of preposition alters the meaning of the verb:

I AGREED TO do what he advised.
I AGREED TO all the conditions.
I AGREED WITH all they said.
See PREPOSITIONS.

agreeable

(*not* agreable)

agreement

For grammatical agreement, see SINGULAR OR PLURAL?.

agressive

Wrong spelling. See AGGRESSIVE.

alga (singular) algae (plural)

See FOREIGN PLURALS.

allege

(*not* -dge)

alley or ally?

An **ALLEY** is a little lane.
An **ALLY** is a friend.
alley (singular), alleys (plural)
ally (singular), allies (plural)
See PLURALS (iii).

all most or almost?

There is a difference in meaning. Use these exemplar sentences as a guide:

They were **ALL** (= everyone) **MOST** kind.
The child was **ALMOST** (= nearly) asleep.

allowed or aloud?

There is a difference in meaning. Use these exemplar sentences as a guide:

Are we **ALLOWED** (= permitted) to smoke in here?
I was just thinking **ALOUD** (= out loud).

all ready or already?

There is a difference in meaning. Use these exemplar sentences as a guide:

We are **ALL** (= everyone) **READY**.
It is **ALL** (= everything) **READY**.
She was **ALREADY** dead (= by then).

all right or alright?

Traditional usage would consider **ALL RIGHT** to be correct and **ALRIGHT** to be incorrect. However, the use of 'alright' is so widespread that some would see it as acceptable although the majority of educated users would take care to avoid it.

all so or also?

There is a difference in meaning. Use these exemplar sentences as a guide:

You are **ALL** (= everyone) **SO** kind.
You are **ALSO** (= in addition) generous.

all together or altogether?

There is a difference in meaning. Use these exemplar sentences as a guide:

They were **ALL** (= everybody) huddled **TOGETHER** for warmth.

→

His situation is **ALTOGETHER** (= totally) different from yours.

allude or elude?

There is a difference in meaning.

ALLUDE means to refer to indirectly.
ELUDE means to evade capture or recall.

allusion, delusion or illusion?

There is a difference in meaning.

An **ALLUSION** is an indirect reference.
A **DELUSION** is a false belief (often associated with a mental disorder).
An **ILLUSION** is a deceptive appearance.

all ways or always?

There is a difference in meaning.

These three routes are **ALL** (= each of them) **WAYS** into town.
She **ALWAYS** (= at all times) tells the truth.

almost

See ALL MOST OR ALMOST?.

a lot

Write as two words, not as one. Bear in mind that this construction is slang and not to be used in a formal context.

aloud

See ALLOWED OR ALOUD?.

already

See ALL READY OR ALREADY?.

altar or alter?

There is a difference in meaning.

The bride and groom stood solemnly before the **ALTAR**.

Do you wish to **ALTER** (= change) the arrangements?

alternate or alternative?

We visit our grandparents on **ALTERNATE** Saturdays. (= every other Saturday)
I **ALTERNATE** between hope and despair. (= have each mood in turn)
An **ALTERNATIVE** plan would be to go by boat. (= another possibility)
The **ALTERNATIVES** are simple: work or go hungry. (= two choices)

alternatives

Strictly speaking, the choice can be between only two alternatives (one choice or the other).

However, the word is frequently used more loosely and this precise definition is becoming lost.

altogether

See **ALL TOGETHER OR ALTOGETHER?**.

Alzheimer's disease

(*not* Alze-)

amateur

(*not* -mm-)

ambiguity

Always try to anticipate any possible confusion on the part of your reader. Check that you have made your meaning absolutely clear.

(i) Bear in mind that pronouns can be very vague. Consider this sentence:

My brother told his friend that **HE** had won first prize in the local photographic exhibition.

Who is 'he', my brother or his friend? Rewrite more clearly:

$\rightarrow$

(a) My brother congratulated his friend on winning first prize in the local photographic exhibition.

(b) My brother, delighted to have won first prize in the local photographic exhibition, told his friend.

The other possibility is rather clumsy but is otherwise clear:

(c) My brother told his friend that he (his friend) had won first prize.

(d) My brother told his friend that he (my brother) had won first prize.

(ii) Position the adverb **ONLY** with great care. It will refer to the word nearest to it, usually the word following. This may not be the meaning you intended. See how crucial to the meaning the position of 'only' can be:

ONLY Sean eats fish on Fridays.
(= No one else but Sean eats fish on Fridays.)

Sean **ONLY** eats fish on Fridays.
(= Sean does nothing else to the fish on Fridays but eat it. He doesn't buy it, cook it, look at it, smell it . . .)

Sean eats **ONLY** fish on Fridays.
(= Sean eats nothing but fish on Fridays.)

Sean eats fish **ONLY** on Fridays.
Sean eats fish on Fridays **ONLY**.
(= Sean eats fish on this one day in the week and never on any other.)

(iii) Take care with the positioning of **BADLY**.

This room needs cleaning **BADLY**.

Does it? Or does it not need cleaning well? Rewrite like this:

This room **BADLY** needs cleaning.

(iv) Beware of causing initial bewilderment by not introducing a comma to indicate a pause.

The shabby little riverside café was empty and full of wasps and flies.

Empty and full?

The shabby little riverside café was empty, and full of wasps and flies.

See COMMAS (ix).

(v) Avoid the danger of writing nonsense!

DRIVING slowly along the road, **THE CASTLE** dominated the landscape.
The castle is driving?

Rewrite:

As we drove slowly along the road, we saw how the castle dominated the landscape.

COOKED slowly, the **FAMILY** will enjoy the cheaper cuts of meat.

Rewrite:

If the cheaper cuts of meat are cooked slowly, the family will enjoy them.

See PARTICIPLES.

(vi) Make sure the descriptive details describe the right noun!

For sale: 1995 Peugeot 205 – one owner with power-assisted steering.

Rewrite:

For sale: 1995 Peugeot 205 with power-assisted steering – one owner.

amend or emend?

Both words mean 'to make changes in order to improve'. Use **AMEND** or **EMEND** when referring to the correction of written or printed text.
Use **AMEND** in a wider context such as **AMENDING** the law or **AMENDING** behaviour.

ammount

Wrong spelling. See AMOUNT.

among

(*not* amoung)

among/amongst

Either form can be used.

among or between?

Use **BETWEEN** when something is shared by two people. Use **AMONG** when it is shared by three or more.

Share the sweets **BETWEEN** the two of you.
Share the sweets **AMONG** yourselves.

However, **BETWEEN** is used with numbers larger than two when it means an exact geographical location or when it refers to relationships.

Sardinia lies **BETWEEN** Spain, Algeria, Corsica and Italy.
It will take a long time before the rift **BETWEEN** the five main parties heals.

amoral or immoral?

There is a difference in meaning.

AMORAL means not being governed by moral laws, acting outside them.
(note -m-)

IMMORAL means breaking the moral laws.
(note -mm-)

amoung
Wrong spelling. See AMONG.

amount
(*not* ammount)

amount or number?
AMOUNT is used with non-count nouns:

a small **AMOUNT** of sugar; a surprising **AMOUNT** of gossip.

NUMBER is used with plural nouns: a **NUMBER** of mistakes; a **NUMBER** of reasons.

analyse
(*not* -ize as in American English)

analysis (singular) analyses (plural)
See FOREIGN PLURALS.

-ance,-ant/-ence,-ent
Words with these endings are difficult to spell and you'll always need to be on your guard with them. Check each word individually when in doubt, but here are some useful guidelines:

(i) People are generally -ant: attendant, lieutenant, occupant, sergeant, tenant (but there are exceptions like superintendent, president, resident ...).

(ii) Use -ance, -ant, where the companion word ends in -ation: dominance, dominant, domination; variance, variant, variation.

(iii) Use -ence, -ent after qu: consequence, consequent; eloquence, eloquent.

(iv) Use -ance, -ant after hard c or hard g: significance, significant (c sounds like k); elegance, elegant (hard g).

→

(v) Use -ence, -ent after soft c or soft g: innocence, innocent (c sounds like s); intelligent, intelligence (g sounds like j).

See SOFT C AND SOFT G.

and/but

Many of us have been taught never to begin a sentence with **AND** or **BUT**. Generally speaking this is good advice. Both words are conjunctions and will therefore be busy joining words within the sentence:

I should love to come **AND** I look forward to the party very much.
They wanted to come **BUT** sadly they had to visit a friend in hospital some miles away.

However, there are some occasions when you may need the extra emphasis that starting a new sentence with **AND** or **BUT** would give. If you have a good reason to break the rules, do so!

anecdote or antidote?

An **ANECDOTE** is a short, amusing account of something that has happened.
An **ANTIDOTE** is a medicine taken to counteract a poison.

angsiety

Wrong spelling. See ANXIETY.

angsious

Wrong spelling. See ANXIOUS.

annex or annexe?

To **ANNEX** is to take possession of a country or part of a country.
An **ANNEX** is another word for an appendix in an official document.
An **ANNEXE** is a building added to the main building.

annoint

Wrong spelling. See ANOINT.

announce

announced, announcing, announcer, announcement (*not* -n-)

annoy

annoyed, annoying, annoyance (*not* anoy or annoied)

annul

annulled, annulling, annulment
See ADDING ENDINGS (iv).

anoint

(*not* -nn-)

anounce

Wrong spelling. See ANNOUNCE.

anoy

Wrong spelling. See ANNOY.

ante-/anti-

ANTE- means before.
antenatal = before birth
ANTI- means against.
antifreeze = against freezing

antecedent

This means earlier in time or an ancestor. (*not* anti-)
See ANTE-/ANTI-.

antediluvian

This means very old-fashioned and primitive, literally 'before the flood of Noah'. (*not* anti-)
See ANTE-/ANTI-.

antenna

This word has two plurals, each used in a different sense:
Use **ANTENNAE** to refer to insects.

→

Use **ANTENNAS** to refer to television aerials.
See FOREIGN PLURALS.

anticlimax
(*not* ante-)
See ANTE-/ANTI-.

antidote
See ANECDOTE OR ANTIDOTE?.

antirrhinum
(*not* -rh-)

antisocial
(*not* ante-)
See ANTE-/ANTI-.

anxiety
(*not* angs-)

anxious
(*not* angs-)

apologise/apologize
Both spellings are correct. (*not* -pp)

apology
apologies (plural)
See PLURALS (iii).

apon
Wrong spelling. See UPON.

apostrophes
(i) Apostrophes can be used to show that letters have been omitted:

◆ *in contractions*
didn't
o'clock
you've
won't

- *in poetry*
  o'er vales and hills
  where'er you walk

- *in dialect*
  'Ere's, 'Arry.

- *in retail*
  pick 'n' mix
  salt 'n' vinegar

(ii) Apostrophes can be used to show ownership.
Follow these simple guidelines and you'll never
put the apostrophe in the wrong place.

Singular nouns or 'owners'
The tail of the dog
The dog's tail

Who 'owns' the tail?	the dog
Put the apostrophe after the owner.	the dog'
Add -s.	the dog's
Add what is 'owned'.	the dog's tail

The smile of the princess
The princess's smile

Who 'owns' the smile?	the princess
Put the apostrophe after the owner.	the princess'
Add -s.	the princess's
Add what is 'owned'.	the princess's smile

With proper names ending in -s, you have a choice,
depending upon how the name is pronounced.

Keats' poetry or Keats's poetry

But St James's Square, London, SW1
St James' (two syllables)
St James's (three syllables)

→

Plural nouns or 'owners'
Don't worry about whether you use 's or s' in the plural. It will sort itself out.

The tails of the dogs
The dogs' tails

Who 'owns' the tails?	the dogs
Put the apostrophe after the owners.	the dogs'
Add -s if there isn't one.	(no need here)
Add what is 'owned'.	the dogs' tails

The laughter of the women
The women's laughter

Who 'owns' the laughter?	the women
Put the apostrophe after the owners.	the women'
Add -s if there isn't one.	the women's
Add what is 'owned'.	the women's laughter

And so, when reading, you will be able to distinguish singular and plural 'owners'.

The princess's suitors.
The princesses' suitors.

The 'owner' is the word before the apostrophe.

(iii) Apostrophes are also used in condensed expressions of time.

The work of a moment.
A moment's work.
The work of three years.
Three years' work.

If you follow the guidelines in (ii) above, you will never make a mistake.

appal
appalled, appalling (*not* -aul-)
See also ADDING ENDINGS (iv).

appearance

(*not* -ence)

appendix

This word has two plurals, each used in a different sense.

Use **APPENDIXES** in an anatomical sense.

Use **APPENDICES** when referring to supplementary sections in books or formal documents.

See also FOREIGN PLURALS.

appologise/-ize

Wrong spelling. See APOLOGISE/APOLOGIZE.

appology

Wrong spelling. See APOLOGY.

appraise or apprise?

To **APPRAISE** is to evaluate.

To **APPRISE** is to inform.

appreciate

There are three distinct meanings of this word.

I **APPRECIATE** your kindness (= recognise gratefully).

I **APPRECIATE** that you have had a difficult time lately (= understand).

My cottage **HAS APPRECIATED** in value already (= increased).

Some people would choose to avoid the second use above (understand, realise) but the verb is now widely used in this sense and this has become acceptable.

approach

approached, approaching (*not* apr-)

aquaint

Wrong spelling. See ACQUAINT.

aquaintance
Wrong spelling. See ACQUAINTANCE.

aquarium (singular) aquaria or aquariums (plural)
See FOREIGN PLURALS.

aquiesce
Wrong spelling. See ACQUIESCE.

aquiescence
Wrong spelling. See ACQUIESCENCE.

aquire
Wrong spelling. See ACQUIRE.

arange
Wrong spelling. See ARRANGE.

arbiter or arbitrator?
An **ARBITER** is a judge or someone with decisive influence (an arbiter of fashion).
In addition, an **ARBITER** may intervene to settle a dispute (-er).
An **ARBITRATOR** is someone who is officially appointed to judge the rights and wrongs of a dispute (-or).

arbitrator or mediator?
An **ARBITRATOR** reaches a judgement but is not necessarily obeyed.
A **MEDIATOR** attempts to bring two opposing sides together and to settle a dispute.

archipelago
There are two interchangeable plural forms: archipelagoes, archipelagos.

arctic
(*not* artic, although frequently mispronounced as such)

argument
(*not* arguement)

arrange
arranged, arranging, arrangement (*not* -r-)
See ADDING ENDINGS (ii).

artefact
American: artifact

artic
Wrong spelling. See ARCTIC.

article
(*not* -cal)
See -CAL/-CLE.

artist or artiste?
Traditionally, an **ARTIST** is skilled in one or more of the fine arts (painting, for example, or sculpture).
Traditionally, the term **ARTISTE** is reserved for a performer or entertainer (a music-hall **ARTISTE**). However, **ARTIST** is now being used to cover both meanings in the sense of 'skilled practitioner', and **ARTISTE** is becoming redundant.

as or like?
Use these exemplar sentences as a guide:

You look **AS** if you have seen a ghost.
You look **AS** though you have seen a ghost.
AS I expected, he's missed the train.
You look **LIKE** your mother.

asma
Wrong spelling. See ASTHMA.

asphalt
(*not* ashphalt, as it is frequently mispronounced)

aspirin
(*not* asprin, as it is frequently mispronounced)

assassin

(*not* assasin or asassin)

assma

Wrong spelling. See ASTHMA.

assume or presume?

To **ASSUME** something to be the case is to take it for granted without any proof.

To **PRESUME** something to be the case is to base it on the evidence available.

assurance or insurance?

Insurance companies distinguish between these two terms.

ASSURANCE is the technical term given for insurance against a certainty (e.g. death) where payment is guaranteed.

INSURANCE is the technical term given for insurance against a risk (such as fire, burglary, illness) where payment is made only if the risk materialises.

asthma

(*not* asma or assma)

astrology or astronomy?

ASTROLOGY is the study of the influence of the stars and planets on human life and fortune.

ASTRONOMY is the scientific study of the stars and planets.

athlete

(*not* athelete)

athletics

(*not* atheletics)

attach

attached, attaching, attachment (*not* -tch)

audible

(*not* -able)

audience
(*not* -ance)

aural or oral?
AURAL refers to the ears and hearing.
ORAL refers to the mouth and speaking.
In speech these words can be very confusing as they are pronounced identically.

authoritative
(*not* authorative)

autobiography or biography?
An **AUTOBIOGRAPHY** is an account of his or her life by the author.

A **BIOGRAPHY** is an account of a life written by someone else.

automaton (singular) automata, automatons (plural)
See FOREIGN PLURALS.

avenge or revenge?
The words are very close in meaning but **AVENGE** is often used in the sense of just retribution, punishing a wrong done to another.

Hamlet felt bound to **AVENGE** his father's death.

REVENGE is often used in the sense of 'getting one's own back' for a petty offence.

averse
See ADVERSE or AVERSE?.

awkward
Notice -wkw-. The spelling itself looks awkward!

axis (singular) axes (plural)
See FOREIGN PLURALS.

B

babyhood
(*not* -i-)
This word is an exception to the -y rule.
See ADDING ENDINGS (iii).

bachelor
(*not* -tch-)

bacillus (singular) bacilli (plural)
See FOREIGN PLURALS.

bacterium (singular) bacteria (plural)
See FOREIGN PLURALS.

badly
This word is often carelessly positioned with
disastrous effects on meaning.
See AMBIGUITY (iii).

banister/bannister
banisters, bannisters (plural)
Although the first spelling is more widely used, both
spellings are correct.

bargain
(*not* -ian)

basically
basic + ally (*not* basicly)

batchelor
Wrong spelling. See BACHELOR.

bath or bathe?
Use these exemplar sentences as a guide:

I have a **BATH** every morning (= I have a wash in
the bath).
I **BATH** the baby every day (= wash in a bath).
I have had a new **BATH** fitted.

We **BATHE** every day (= swim).
BATHE the wound with disinfectant (= cleanse).
We have a **BATHE** whenever we can (= a swim).

beach or beech?

Use these exemplar sentences as a guide:

Budleigh Salterton has a stony **BEACH**.
BEECH trees shed their leaves in autumn.

beautiful

Use your knowledge of French *beau* to help you.

before

(*not* befor)

begin

Note these forms and spellings:

I begin, I am beginning.
I began, I have begun.

beginner

(*not* -n-)

beige

(*not* -ie-)
See EI/IE SPELLING RULE.

belief

(*not* -ei)
See EI/IE SPELLING RULE.

believe

believed, believing, believer
See EI/IE SPELLING RULE.
See ADDING ENDINGS (ii).

benefit

benefited, benefiting
It is a common mistake to use -tt-.

berth or birth?

Use these exemplar sentences as a guide:

We have a spare **BERTH** on our boat.
We are proud to announce the **BIRTH** of a daughter.

beside or besides?

Use **BESIDE** in the sense of next to, by the side of:

Your glasses are **BESIDE** your bed.
May I sit **BESIDE** you?

Use **BESIDES** in the sense of also, as well as:

BESIDES, I can't afford it.
BESIDES being very clever, Ann also works hard.

between

See AMONG OR BETWEEN?.

between you and I

Incorrect. Write: between you and me.
See PREPOSITIONS.

bi-

This prefix means 'two'.
Hence bicycle
    bifocals
    bigamy, and so on.
Note, however, that some words beginning with 'bi' can be ambiguous.
See BIMONTHLY and BIWEEKLY.
See also BIANNUAL OR BIENNIAL?.

biannual or biennial?

BIANNUAL means twice a year (*not* -n-).
BIENNIAL means every two years (a biennial festival) or lasting for two years (horticultural, etc). (*not* -ual)

bicycle
bi + cycle
(*not* bycycle or bycicle)

bidding or biding?
bid + ing = bidding

The **BIDDING** at the auction was fast and furious.
BIDDING farewell, the knight cantered away.

bide + ing = biding

Her critics were just **BIDING** their time.
See ADDING ENDINGS (i) and (ii).

biege
Wrong spelling. See BEIGE.

biennial
See BIANNUAL OR BIENNIAL?.

bimonthly
Avoid using **BIMONTHLY** as it has two conflicting meanings. It can mean both every two months and also twice a month. (Compare BIWEEKLY.)

binoculars
(*not* -nn-)

biography
See AUTOBIOGRAPHY OR BIOGRAPHY?.

biscuit
(*not* -iu-)

biulding
Wrong spelling. See BUILDING.

bivouac
bivouacked, bivouacking
See SOFT C AND SOFT G.

biweekly
This word has two conflicting meanings and is

→

perhaps best avoided. It can mean both every two weeks (i.e. fortnightly) and also twice a week. (Compare BIMONTHLY.)

bizarre

(*not* -zz-)

blond or blonde?

BLOND is used to describe men's hair.
BLOND/BLONDE is used to describe women's hair.
A **BLONDE** is a woman.

board or bored?

A **BOARD** is a piece of wood, also a committee or similar group of people.
To **BOARD** means to get on (train, etc.) and also to pay for living in someone's house and having food provided.
BORED means uninterested.

boarder or border?

A **BOARDER** is a person who pays to live in someone's house or school.
A **BORDER** is the edge or boundary of something.

boisterous

(*not* boistrous, although often mispronounced as two syllables)

boney/bony

Both spellings are correct, although the second spelling is more commonly used.

border

See BOARDER OR BORDER?.

bored

See BOARD OR BORED?.

bored by, bored with

(*not* bored of)

born or borne?

Use these exemplar sentences as a guide:

Dickens was **BORN** in Portsmouth.
She has **BORNE** five children.
He has **BORNE** a heavy burden of guilt all his life.

borrow or lend?

May I **BORROW** your pen? (= use your pen temporarily)
Please **LEND** me your pen. (= pass it to me and allow me to use it)

both... and

Take care with the positioning of each half of this paired construction. Each must introduce grammatically similar things:

He is **BOTH** clever **AND** hardworking.
(*not*: He both is clever and hardworking!)

He **BOTH** paints **AND** sculpts.
He bought **BOTH** the gardening tools **AND** the DIY kit.

Notice, however, the ambiguity in the last example. It could mean that there were just two gardening tools and he bought both of them. In the case of possible confusion, always replace:

He bought the gardening tools and also the DIY kit.
He bought the two gardening tools and also the DIY kit.
He bought both of the gardening tools and also the DIY kit.

bought or brought?

BOUGHT is the past tense of to buy.

She **BOUGHT** eggs, bacon and bread.

BROUGHT is the past tense of to bring.

→

They **BROUGHT** their books home.

bouncy
>(*not* -ey)
>See ADDING ENDINGS (ii).

brackets
>Round brackets enclose additional information which the writer wants to keep separate from the main body of the sentence.

>Jane Austen (born in 1775) died in Winchester.
>My neighbour (have you met her?) has won £250,000.

>Notice how sentences in brackets are not fully punctuated.
>   They don't begin with a capital letter or have a full stop at the end if they occur within another sentence as in the example above. They do, however, have a question mark or an exclamation mark, if appropriate.
>   Square brackets indicate that the material has been added to the original by another writer:

>When I [Hilaire Belloc] am dead, I hope it may be said:
>'His sins were scarlet, but his books were read.'

breath or breathe?
>**BREATH** is the noun, and rhymes with 'death'.

>He called for help with his dying **BREATH**.

>**BREATHE** is the verb and rhymes with 'seethe'.

>**BREATHE** deeply and fill those lungs!

brief, briefly
>(*not* -ei-)

Britain
>(*not* -ian)

Brittany
(*not* Britanny)

broach or brooch?
You **BROACH** a difficult topic or **BROACH** a bottle.
You wear a **BROOCH**.

broccoli
(*not* brocolli)

broken
(*not* brocken)

brought
See **BOUGHT OR BROUGHT?**.

buffalo (singular) buffaloes (plural)
See **PLURALS** (iv).

building
(*not* -iu-)

buisness
Wrong spelling. See **BUSINESS**.

bureau
bureaux, bureaus (plural)
Both forms are correct.
See **FOREIGN PLURALS**.

bureaucracy
(*not* -sy)

burglar
(*not* burgular, as often mispronounced)

burned/burnt
Both forms are correct.

business
(*not* buisness)

but
See **AND/BUT**.

buy/by

Use these exemplar sentences as a guide:

I need to **BUY** some new jeans.
The book is **BY** Charlotte Brontë.
Wait **BY** the gate.
The children rushed **BY**.

C

cactus (singular) cactuses or cacti (plural)
See FOREIGN PLURALS.

caffeine
(*not* -ie-)

-cal/-cle
Adjectives end in -cal.
Nouns end in -cle.

e.g.	critical	article
	logical	bicycle
	magical	circle
	musical	cubicle
	nautical	cuticle
	physical	miracle
	practical	particle
	theatrical	spectacle
	tropical	uncle
	whimsical	vehicle

calculator
(*not* -er)

calendar

calf (singular) calves (plural)
See PLURALS (v).

callous or callus?
CALLOUS means cruel, insensitive, not caring about how others feel.
CALLUS means a hard patch of skin or tissue.
Interestingly, skin may be CALLOUSED (made hard) or CALLUSED (having calluses).

can or may?
Strictly speaking, CAN means 'being able' and MAY means 'having permission'. It is best to preserve this

→

distinction in formal contexts. However, informally, **CAN** is used to cover both meanings:

You **CAN** go now (= are permitted).

caning or canning?

cane + ing = caning

CANING is now banned in all schools.

Can + ing = canning

The **CANNING** factory is closing down.
See ADDING ENDINGS (i) and (ii).

canister

(*not* -nn-)

cannon or canon?

A **CANON** is a cleric.

A **CANNON** is a large gun.

cannot or can not?

Both forms are acceptable but the second is rarely seen.

canoe

canoed, canoeing, canoeist
See ADDING ENDINGS (ii).

canon

See CANNON OR CANON?.

can't

Contraction of **CANNOT**.

canvas or canvass?

CANVAS is a rough cloth.
To **CANVASS** is to ask for votes.

capital letters

Use a capital letter in these circumstances:

◆ to begin a sentence:

My father will be fifty tomorrow.

◆ to begin sentences of direct speech:

'You will be sorry for this in the morning,' she said.
She said, 'You will be sorry for this in the morning. You never learn.'

◆ for the pronoun 'I' wherever it comes in the sentence:

You know that I have no money.

◆ for all proper nouns – names of:

people (Mary Browne)
countries (Malta)
languages (French)
religious festivals (Easter, Diwali)
firms (Express Cleaners)
organisations (the British Broadcasting
                       Corporation)
historical periods (the Renaissance)
                       (the Neolithic Period)
days of the week (Monday)
months of the year (September)
                  but not usually the seasons

Note these adjectives derived from proper nouns also have a capital letter:

a Jewish festival; a German poet

However, the capital is dropped when the connection with the proper noun becomes lost:

venetian blinds, french windows

Note also that titles are capitalised only when part of a proper noun:

Bishop Christopher Budd, otherwise the bishop
Aunt Gladys, otherwise my aunt

→

Captain Llewellyn, otherwise the captain

◆ to begin lines of poetry (although some poets like e.e. cummings dispense with this convention)

◆ to mark the first word and the subsequent key words in titles:

The Taming of the Shrew
An Old Wives' Tale

◆ for emphasis:

And then – BANG!

◆ for some acronyms and initialisms:
NATO
UNESCO
CAFOD
OXFAM
PTO
RSVP

Note that some acronyms have now become words in their own right and are no longer written in capitals: laser, sauna, radar.

Note also that some initialisms are usually written in lower case: i.e., e.g., c/o, wpm.

◆ for the Deity as a mark of respect and for sacred books:

God, Jesus Christ, the Holy Spirit, the Almighty, Allah, Jehovah, Yahweh
the Bible, the Koran, the Vedas

◆ to begin each word in an address:

Mrs Anna Sendall
10 Furze Crescent
ALPHINGTON
Hants PD6 9EF

◆ for the salutation in a letter (first word and key words only) and for the first letter of the complimentary close:

Dear Sir
Dear Mrs Hughes
My dear niece
Yours faithfully
Yours sincerely
With much love
With best wishes

capital punishment or corporal punishment?
CAPITAL PUNISHMENT = death
CORPORAL PUNISHMENT = beating

cappuccino
(*not* -p-)

capsize
This is the *only* verb in the English language of more than one syllable that *must* end in -ize.

captain
(*not* -ian)

capuccino
Wrong spelling. See CAPPUCCINO.

career
(*not* -rr-)

cargo (singular) cargoes (plural)
See PLURALS (iv).

Caribbean
(*not* -rr-, *not* -b-)

carreer
Wrong spelling. See CAREER.

carrying
carry + ing

→

See **ADDING ENDINGS** (iii).

cast or caste?

Use **CAST** for a group of actors in a play and for a plaster **CAST** and a **CAST** in an eye.
Use **CASTE** when referring to a social group in Hindu society.

caster or castor?

Both caster sugar and castor sugar are correct.
Both sugar caster and sugar castor are correct.
Both casters and castors can be used when referring to the little wheels fixed to the legs of furniture.
But castor oil, *not* caster oil.

catagorical

Wrong spelling. See **CATEGORICAL**.

catagory

Wrong spelling. See **CATEGORY**.

catarrh

(*not* -rh)

catastrophe

(*not* -y)

categorical

categorically (*not* cata-)

category (singular) categories (plural) (*not* cata-)
cauliflower

(*not* -flour)

ceiling

(*not* -ie-)
See **EI/IE SPELLING RULE**.

Cellophane

(*not* Sello-)

censer, censor or censure?

A **CENSER** is a container in which incense is burnt during a religious ceremony.

A **CENSOR** is a person who examines plays, books, films, etc. before deciding if they are suitable for public performance or publication.
To **CENSOR** is to do the work of a **CENSOR**.

CENSURE is official and formal disapproval or condemnation of an action.
To **CENSURE** is to express this condemnation in a formal written or spoken statement.

centenarian or centurion?

A **CENTENARIAN** is someone who is at least 100 years old.
A **CENTURION** is the commander of a company of 100 men in the ancient Roman army.

century (singular) centuries (plural) (*not* centua-)
See PLURALS (iii).

cereal or serial?

CEREAL is food processed from grain.
A **SERIAL** is a book or radio or television performance delivered in instalments.

ceremonial or ceremonious?

Both adjectives come from the noun **CEREMONY**.
CEREMONIAL describes the ritual used for a formal religious or public event (a **CEREMONIAL** occasion).
CEREMONIOUS describes the type of person who likes to behave over-formally on social occasions. It is not altogether complimentary (a **CEREMONIOUS** wave of the hand).

ceremony (singular) ceremonies (plural)
See PLURALS (iii).

certain or curtain

CERTAIN means sure.

Are you **CERTAIN** that he apologised?

CURTAINS are window drapes.

Do draw the **CURTAINS**.

Note that the c sounds like s in certain and like k in curtain.
See SOFT C AND SOFT G.

changeable

(*not* -gable)
See SOFT C AND SOFT G.

chaos

chaotic

character

(*not* charachter)

chateau/château (singular) chateaux or châteaux (plural)

See FOREIGN PLURALS.

check or cheque?

Use these exemplar sentences as a guide:

Always **CHECK** your work.
May I pay by **CHEQUE**? (*not* 'check' as in the United States)

cherub (singular)

This word has two plurals.
Cherubim is reserved exclusively for the angels often portrayed as little children with wings.
Cherubs can be used either for angels or for enchanting small children.

chestnut

(*not* chesnut, as it is often mispronounced)

chief (singular) chiefs (plural)
See PLURALS (v).

childish or childlike?
The teenager was rebuked by the magistrate for his
CHILDISH behaviour. (i.e. which he should have
outgrown)
The grandfather has retained his sense of
CHILDLIKE wonder at the beauty of the natural
world. (i.e. marvellously direct, innocent and
enthusiastic)

chimney (singular) chimneys (plural)
See PLURALS (iii).

chior
Wrong spelling. See CHOIR.

chocolate
(*not* choclat although often mispronounced as such)

choice
(*not* -se)

choir
(*not* -io-)

choose
I **CHOOSE** my words carefully.
I am **CHOOSING** my words carefully.
I **CHOSE** my words carefully yesterday.
I have **CHOSEN** them carefully.

chord or cord?
CHORD is used in a mathematical or musical
context.
CORD refers to string and is generally used when
referring to anatomical parts like the umbilical cord,
spinal cord and vocal cords.
Note: you will occasionally see **CHORD** used instead
of **CORD** in a medical context but it seems very old-
fashioned now.

Christianity
(*not* Cr-)

Christmas
(*not* Cristmas or Chrismas)

chronic
(*not* cr-)
This word is often misused. It doesn't mean terrible or serious. It means long-lasting, persistent, when applied to an illness.

chrysanthemum
(*not* cry-)

chrystal
Wrong spelling. See CRYSTAL.

cieling
Wrong spelling. See CEILING.

cigarette
(*not* -rr)

cite, sight or site?
To **CITE** means to refer to.
SIGHT is vision or something seen.
A **SITE** is land, usually set aside for a particular purpose.

clarity
See AMBIGUITY.

clothes or cloths?
CLOTHES are garments.
CLOTHS are dusters or scraps of material.

coarse or course?
COARSE means vulgar, rough:
COARSE language, **COARSE** cloth.

COURSE means certainly:

OF COURSE

COURSE also means a series of lectures, a direction, a sports area, and part of a meal:

an advanced **COURSE**
to change **COURSE**
a golf **COURSE**
the main **COURSE**

codeine
(*not* -ie-)

colander
(*not* -ar)

collaborate
collaborated, collaborating

collaborator
collaboration

collapse
collapsed, collapsing

collapsible
(*not* -able)

colleagues

collective nouns
See NOUNS.

college
(*not* colledge)

colloquial

collossal
Wrong spelling. See COLOSSAL.

colonel or kernel?
A **COLONEL** is a senior officer.
A **KERNEL** is the inner part of a nut.

colons

    (i)   Colons can introduce a list:

        Get your ingredients together:
flour, sugar, dried fruit, butter and milk.

        Note that a summing-up word should always precede the colon (here 'ingredients').

    (ii)   Colons can precede an explanation or amplification of what has gone before:

        The teacher was elated: at last the pupils were gaining in confidence.

        Note that what precedes the colon must always be able to stand on its own grammatically. It must be a sentence in its own right.

    (iii)   Colons can introduce dialogue in a play:

        Henry (with some embarrassment): It's all my own fault.

    (iv)   Colons can be used instead of a comma to introduce direct speech:

        Henry said, with some embarrassment: 'It's all my own fault.'

    (v)   Colons can introduce quotations:

        Donne closes the poem with the moving tribute:
'Thy firmness makes my circle just
And makes me end where I began.'

    (vi)   Colons can introduce examples as in this reference book.

        Compare SEMICOLONS.

colossal

    (*not* -ll-)

colour

(*not* color, as in American English)

colourful

comemorate

Wrong spelling. See COMMEMORATE.

comfortable

(four syllables, not three)

coming

come + ing = coming (*not* comming)
See ADDING ENDINGS (ii).

comission

Wrong spelling. See COMMISSION.

commands

(i) Direct commands, if expressed emphatically, require an exclamation mark:

Stop, thief!
Put your hands up!
Stop talking!

If expressed calmly and conversationally, however, a full stop is sufficient:

Just wait there a moment and I'll be with you.
Tell me your story once again.

(ii) Reported commands (indirect commands) never need an exclamation mark because, when they are reported, they become statements.

He ordered the thief to stop.
She told him to put his hands up.
The teacher yelled at the class to stop talking.

commas

Commas are so widely misused that it is worth discussing their function in some detail. First, let us make it very clear when commas *cannot* be used. →

(a) A comma should never divide a subject from its verb. The two go together:

My parents, had very strict views. ✗
My parents had very strict views. ✓

Take extra care with compound subjects:

The grandparents, the parents, and the children, were in some ways to blame. ✗
The grandparents, the parents, and the children were in some ways to blame. ✓

(b) Commas should never be used in an attempt to string sentences together. Sentences must be either properly joined (and commas don't have this function) or clearly separated by full stops, question marks or exclamation marks.

Commas have certain very specific jobs to do within a sentence. Let us look at each in turn:

(i) Commas separate items in a list:

I bought apples, pears, and grapes.
She washed up, made the beds, and had breakfast.
The novel is funny, touching, and beautifully written.

The final comma before 'and' in a list is optional. However, use it to avoid any ambiguity. See (ix) below.

(ii) Commas are used to separate terms of address from the rest of the sentence:

Sheila, how nice to see you!
Can I help you, madam?
I apologise, ladies and gentlemen, for this delay.

Note that a pair of commas is needed in the last example above because the term of address occurs mid-sentence. It is a very common error to omit one of the commas.

(iii) Commas are used to separate interjections, asides and sentence tags like isn't it? don't you? haven't you?. You'll notice in the examples below that all these additions could be removed and these sentences would still be grammatically sound:

My mother, despite her good intentions, soon stopped going to the gym.
Of course, I'll help you when I can.
You've met Tom, haven't you?

(iv) Commas are used to mark off phrases in apposition:

Prince Charles, the future king, has an older sister.

The phrase 'the future king' is another way of referring to 'Prince Charles' and is punctuated just like an aside.

(v) A comma separates any material that precedes it from the main part of the sentence:

Although she admired him, she would never go out with him.
If you want to read the full story, buy *The Sunday Times*.

Note that if the sentences are reversed so that the main part of the sentence comes first, the comma becomes optional.

(vi) Commas mark off participles and participial phrases, whenever they come in the sentence:

Laughing gaily, she ran out of the room.
He flung himself on the sofa, overcome with remorse.
The children, whispering excitedly, crowded

→

through the door.

For a definition of participles see PARTICIPLES.

(vii) Commas mark off some adjectival clauses. Don't worry too much about the grammatical terminology here. You'll be able to decide whether you need to mark them off in your own work by matching them against these examples.

Can you see the difference in meaning that a pair of commas makes here? Read the two sentences aloud, pausing where the commas indicate that you should pause in the first sentence, and the two different meanings should become clear:

The firemen, who wore protective clothing, were uninjured. (= nobody injured)

The firemen who wore protective clothing were uninjured. (but those who didn't wear it . . .)

(viii) Commas are used to mark a pause at a suitable point in a long sentence. This will be very much a question of style. Read your own work carefully and decide exactly how you want it to be read.

(ix) Commas are sometimes needed to clarify meaning. In the examples below, be aware how the reader could initially make an inappropriate connection:
She reversed the car into the main road and my brother waved goodbye.
She reversed the car into the main road and my brother??
She reversed the car into the main road, and my brother waved goodbye.

In the skies above the stars glittered palely.
In the skies above the stars??
In the skies above, the stars glittered palely.

Notice how the comma can sometimes be essential with 'and' in a list:

We shopped at Moores, Browns, Supervalu, Marks and Spencer and Leonards.

Is the fourth shop called Marks, or Marks and Spencer?
Is the fifth shop called Leonards, or Spencer and Leonards?

A comma makes all clear:

We shopped at Moores, Browns, Supervalu, Marks and Spencer, and Leonards.

commemorate
> (*not* -m-)

comming
> Wrong spelling. See COMING.

commission
> (*not* -m-)

commit
> committed, committing, commitment
> See ADDING ENDINGS (iv).

committee

common nouns
> See NOUNS.

comparative
> comparatively (*not* compari-)

comparative and superlative
> (i)   Use the comparative form of adjectives and adverbs when comparing two:

→

John is **TALLER** than Tom.
John works **MORE ENERGETICALLY** than Tom.

Use the superlative form when comparing three or more:

John is the **TALLEST** of all the engineers.
John works **THE MOST ENERGETICALLY** of all the engineers.

(ii) There are two ways of forming the comparative and superlative of adjectives:

(a) Add -er and -est to short adjectives:

tall	taller	tallest
happy	happier	happiest

(b) Use more and most with longer adjectives:

dangerous	more dangerous	most dangerous
successful	more successful	most successful

The comparative and superlative forms of adverbs are formed in exactly the same way:

(c) Short adverbs add -er and -est.

You run **FASTER** than I do.
He runs the **FASTEST** of us all.

(d) Use more and most with longer adverbs.

Nikki works **MORE CONSCIENTIOUSLY** than Sarah.
Niamh works **THE MOST CONSCIENTIOUSLY** of them all.

(iii) There are three irregular adjectives:

good	better	best
bad	worse	worst
many	more	most

There are four irregular adverbs:

well	better	best
badly	worse	worst
much	more	most
little	less	least

(iv) A very common error is to mix the two methods of forming the comparative and the superlative:

more simpler ✗ simpler ✓
most easiest ✗ easiest ✓

(v) Another pitfall is to try to form the comparative and superlative of absolute words like perfect, unique, excellent, complete, ideal. Something is either perfect or it isn't. It can't be more perfect or less perfect, most perfect or least perfect.

compare to/compare with
Both constructions are acceptable but many people still prefer to use 'compare with'.

comparitive
Wrong spelling. See COMPARATIVE.

competition
competitive, competitively

complacent or complaisant?
COMPLACENT = smug, self-satisfied
COMPLAISANT = obliging, willing to comply

compleatly
Wrong spelling. See COMPLETELY.

complement or compliment?
COMPLEMENT = that which completes
Half the ship's **COMPLEMENT** were recruited in Norway.
To **COMPLEMENT** = to go well with something
Her outfit was **COMPLEMENTED** by well-chosen accessories.

COMPLIMENT = praise, flattering remarks

→

To **COMPLIMENT** = to praise

complementary or complimentary?

Use **COMPLEMENTARY** in the sense of completing a whole:

COMPLEMENTARY medicine
COMPLEMENTARY jobs

Use **COMPLIMENTARY** in two senses:

(a) flattering
(b) free of charge

COMPLIMENTARY remarks
COMPLIMENTARY tickets

completely

complete + ly (*not* completly, completley or compleatly)
See ADDING ENDINGS (ii).

complex or complicated?

Both words mean 'made up of many different intricate and confusing aspects'. However, use **COMPLEX** when you mean 'intricate', and **COMPLICATED** when you mean 'difficult to understand'.

compliment

See COMPLEMENT OR COMPLIMENT?.

compose/comprise

The report **IS COMPOSED OF** ten sections. (= is made up of)
The report **COMPRISES** ten sections. (= contains)

Never use the construction 'is comprised of'. It is always incorrect grammatically.

comprise

(*not* -ize)

compromise
(*not* -ize)

computer
(*not* -or)

concede

conceive
conceived, conceiving, conceivable
See EI/IE SPELLING RULE.

concise

confer
conferred, conferring, conference
See ADDING ENDINGS (iv).

confidant, confidante or confident?
A **CONFIDANT** (male or female) or a **CONFIDANTE**
(female only) is someone to whom one tells one's
secrets 'in confidence'.
CONFIDENT means assured.

connection or connexion?
Both spellings are correct, but the first one is more
commonly used.

connoisseur
Used for both men and women.

conscientious

consist in or consist of?
For Belloc, happiness **CONSISTED IN** 'laughter and
the love of friends'. (consist in = have as its
essence)

Lunch **CONSISTED OF** bread, cheese and fruit.

consistent
(*not* -ant)

consonant

There are 21 consonants in the alphabet, all the letters except for the vowels:

bcdfghjklmnpqrstvwxyz

Note, however, that y can be both a vowel and a consonant:

y is a consonant when it begins a word or a syllable (yolk, beyond);
y is a vowel when it sounds like i or e (sly, baby).

contagious or infectious?

Both refer to diseases passed to others.
Strictly speaking, **CONTAGIOUS** means passed by bodily contact, and **INFECTIOUS** means passed by means of air or water.
Used figuratively, the terms are interchangeable:

INFECTIOUS laughter, **CONTAGIOUS** enthusiasm.

contemporary

(*not* contempory, as often mispronounced)
Nowadays, this word is used in two senses:

(a) happening or living at the same time (in the past)
(b) modern, current

Be aware of possible ambiguity if both these meanings are possible in a given context:

Hamlet is being performed in contemporary dress.
(sixteenth-century or modern?)

contemptible or contemptuous

A person or an action worthy of contempt is **CONTEMPTIBLE**.
A person who shows contempt is **CONTEMPTUOUS**.

continual

continually

continual or continuous?

CONTINUAL means frequently repeated, occurring with short breaks only.

CONTINUOUS means uninterrupted.

contractions

Take care with placing the apostrophe in contractions. It is placed where the letter has been omitted and not where the two words are joined. These happen to coincide in some contractions:

I'd (I would)
they aren't (they are not)
it isn't (it is not)
you hadn't (you had not)
you wouldn't (you would not)
she won't (she will not)
we haven't (we have not)
I shan't (I shall not)

It was common in Jane Austen's time to use two apostrophes in shan't (sha'n't) to show that two sets of letters had been omitted but this is no longer correct today.

control

controlled, controlling

controller

(*not* -or)

convenience

(*not* -ance)

convenient

conveniently (*not* convien-)

cord

See CHORD OR CORD?.

corporal punishment

See CAPITAL OR CORPORAL PUBLISHMENT?.

correspond

(*not* -r-)

correspondence

(*not* -ance)

correspondent or co-respondent?

A **CORRESPONDENT** is someone who writes letters.

A **CO-RESPONDENT** is cited in divorce proceedings.

could of

This is incorrect and arises from an attempt to write down what is heard. Write 'could've' in informal contexts and 'could have' in formal ones.

I **COULD HAVE** given you a lift.
I **COULD'VE** given you a lift.

Beware also: should of/would of/must of/might of. All are incorrect forms.

couldn't

See CONTRACTIONS.

council or counsel?

A **COUNCIL** is a board of elected representatives. **COUNSEL** is advice, also the term used for a barrister representing a client in court.

councillor or counsellor?

A **COUNCILLOR** is an elected representative.
A **COUNSELLOR** is one who gives professional guidance, such as a study **COUNSELLOR**, a marriage **COUNSELLOR**, a debt **COUNSELLOR**.

counterfeit

This is one of the few exceptions to the IE/EI spelling rule.
See IE/EI SPELLING RULE.

courageous
(*not* -gous)
See SOFT C AND SOFT G.

course
See COARSE OR COURSE?.

courteous
courteously, courtesy

credible or credulous?
If something is **CREDIBLE**, it is believable.

If someone is **CREDULOUS**, he or she is gullible (i.e. too easily taken in).

crisis (singular) crises (plural)
See FOREIGN PLURALS.

criterion (singular) criteria (plural)
See FOREIGN PLURALS.

criticise/criticize
Both spellings are correct.

criticism
This word is frequently misspelt.
Remember critic + ism.

cronic
Wrong spelling. See CHRONIC.

crucial

cry
cried, crying
See ADDING ENDINGS (iii).

crysanthemum
Wrong spelling. See CHRYSANTHEMUM.

crystal
(*not* chr-)

cupboard

(*not* cub-)

curb or kerb

To **CURB** one's temper means to control or restrain it.

A **CURB** is a restraint (e.g. a curb bit for a horse).

A **KERB** is the edging of a pavement.

curious

curiosity

(*not* -ious-)

curly

(*not* -ey)

currant or current?

A **CURRANT** is a small dried grape used in cooking.

A **CURRENT** is a steady flow of water, air or electricity.

CURRENT can also mean happening at the present time (as in **CURRENT** affairs, **CURRENT** practice).

curriculum (singular) curriculums/curricula (plural)

See FOREIGN PLURALS.

curriculum vitae

(abbreviation: CV)

curtain

See CERTAIN OR CURTAIN?.

daily

(*not* dayly)
This is an exception to the -y rule.
See ADDING ENDINGS (iii).

dairy or diary?

We buy our cream at a local **DAIRY**.
Kate writes in her **DIARY** every day.

dangling participles

See PARTICIPLES.

dashes

Dashes are used widely in informal notes and letters.

(i) A dash can be used to attach an afterthought:

I should love to come – that's if I can get the time off.

(ii) A dash can replace a colon before a list in informal writing:

The thieves took everything – video, television, cassettcs, computer, camera, the lot.

(iii) A dash can precede a summary:

Video, television, cassettes, computer, camera – the thieves took the lot.

(iv) A pair of dashes can be used like a pair of commas or a pair of brackets around a parenthesis:

Geraldine is – as you know – very shy with strangers.

(v) A dash can mark a pause before the climax is reached:

There he was at the foot of the stairs – dead. →

(vi) Dashes can indicate hesitation in speech:

I – er – don't – um – know what – what to say.

(vii) Dashes can indicate missing letters or even missing words where propriety or discretion require it:

c – – – l (ship of the desert)
Susan L— comes from Exeter.
He swore softly, ' ——— it'.

data (plural) datum (singular)
Strictly speaking, **DATA** should be used with a plural verb:

The **DATA** have been collected by research students.

You will, however, increasingly see **DATA** used with a singular verb and this use has now become acceptable.

The **DATA** has been collected by research students.

dates
See NUMBERS for a discussion of how to set out dates.

deceased or diseased?
DECEASED means dead.
DISEASED means affected by illness or infection.

deceit
(*not* -ie)
See EI/IE SPELLING RULE.

deceive

decent or descent?
DECENT means fair, upright, reasonable.
DESCENT means act of coming down, ancestry.

decide
decided, deciding (*not* decied-)

deciet
Wrong spelling. See DECEIT.

decieve
Wrong spelling. See DECEIVE.

decision

décolletage
(*not* de-)

decrepit
(*not* -id)

defective or deficient?
DEFECTIVE means not working properly (a
DEFECTIVE machine).
DEFICIENT means lacking something vital (a diet
DEFICIENT in vitamin C).

defer
deferred, deferring, deference
See ADDING ENDINGS (iv).

deffinite
Wrong spelling. See DEFINITE.

deficient
See DEFECTIVE OR DEFICIENT?.

definate
Wrong spelling. See DEFINITE.

definite
(*not* -ff-, *not* -ate)

definitely

deisel
Wrong spelling. See DIESEL.

delapidated
Wrong spelling. See DILAPIDATED.

delusion

See ALLUSION, DELUSION OR ILLUSION?.

denouement/dénouement

Both spellings are correct.

dependant or dependent?

The adjective (meaning reliant) is always -ent.

She is a widow with five **DEPENDENT** children.
I am absolutely **DEPENDENT** on a pension.

The noun (meaning someone who is dependent) has traditionally been spelt -ant. However, the American practice of writing either -ant or -ent for the noun has now spread here. Either spelling is now considered correct for the noun but be aware that some conservative readers would consider this slipshod.

She has five **DEPENDANTS/DEPENDENTS**.

descent

See DECENT OR DESCENT?.

describe

(*not* dis-)

description

(*not* -scrib-)

desease

Wrong spelling. See DISEASE.

desert or dessert?

A **DESERT** is sandy.
A **DESSERT** is a pudding.

desiccated

(*not* dess-)

desirable

(*not* desireable)
See ADDING ENDINGS (ii).

desperate

(*not* desparate)
The word is derived from *spes* (Latin word for hope). This may help you to remember the e in the middle syllable.

dessert

See DESERT OR DESSERT?.

dessiccated

Wrong spelling. See DESICCATED.

destroy

destroyed, destroying (*not* dis-)
See ADDING ENDINGS (iii).

detached

(*not* detatched)

deter

deterred, deterring
See ADDING ENDINGS (iv).

deteriorate

(*not* deteriate, as it is often mispronounced)

deterrent

(*not* -ant)

develop

developed, developing (*not* -pp-)

development

(*not* developement)

device/devise

DEVICE is the noun.

A padlock is an intriguing DEVICE.

→

DEVISE is the verb.

Try to **DEVISE** a simple burglar alarm.

diagnosis (singular) diagnoses (plural)
See FOREIGN PLURALS.

diagnosis or prognosis?
DIAGNOSIS is the identification of an illness or a difficulty.
PROGNOSIS is the forecast of its likely development and effects.

diarrhoea

diary (singular) diaries (plural)
See PLURALS (iii).
See DAIRY OR DIARY?.

dictionary (singular) dictionaries (plural) (*not* -nn-)
See PLURALS (iii).

didn't
(*not* did'nt)
See CONTRACTIONS.

diesel
(*not* deisel)
See EI/IE SPELLING RULE.

dietician/dietitian
Both spellings are correct.

differcult
Wrong spelling. See DIFFICULT.

difference
(*not* -ance)

different
(*not* -ant)

different from/to/than
'Different from' and 'different to' are now both

considered acceptable forms.

My tastes are **DIFFERENT FROM** yours.
My tastes are **DIFFERENT TO** yours.

Conservative users would, however, much prefer the preposition 'from' and this is widely used in formal contexts.

'Different than' is acceptable in American English but is not yet fully acceptable in British English.

difficult

(*not* differcult, *not* difficalt)

dilapidated

(*not* delapidated)

dilemma

This word is often used loosely to mean 'a problem'. Strictly speaking it means a difficult choice between two possibilities.

dinghy or dingy?

A **DINGHY** is a boat (plural – dinghies).
See PLURALS (iii).
DINGY means dull and drab.

dingo (singular) dingoes or dingos (plural)

dining or dinning?

dine + ing = dining (as in dining room)
din + ing = dinning (noise dinning in ears)
See ADDING ENDINGS (i) and (ii).

diphtheria

(*not* diptheria as it is often mispronounced)

diphthong

(*not* dipthong as it is often mispronounced)

direct speech

See INVERTED COMMAS.

disagreeable
dis + agree + able

disappear
dis + appear

disappearance
(*not* -ence)

disappoint
dis + appoint

disapprove
dis + approve

disassociate or dissociate?
Both are correct, but the second is more widely used and approved.

disaster

disastrous
(*not* disasterous, as it is often mispronounced)

disc or disk?
Use 'disc' except when referring to computer disks.

disciple
(*not* disiple)

discipline

discover or invent?
You **DISCOVER** something that has been there all the time unknown to you (e.g. a star).
You **INVENT** something if you create it for the first time (e.g. a time machine).

discreet or discrete?
You are **DISCREET** if you can keep secrets and behave diplomatically.
Subject areas are **DISCRETE** if they are quite separate and unrelated.

discrepancy (singular) discrepancies (plural)

discribe
Wrong spelling. See DESCRIBE.

discribtion
Wrong spelling. See DESCRIPTION.

discription
Wrong spelling. See DESCRIPTION.

discuss
discussed, discussing

discussion

disease

diseased
See DECEASED OR DISEASED?.

dishevelled

disintegrate
(*not* disintergrate)

disinterested or uninterested?
Careful users would wish to preserve a distinction in meaning between these two words. Use the word **DISINTERESTED** to mean 'impartial, unselfish, acting for the good of others and not for yourself'.

My motives are entirely **DISINTERESTED**; it is justice I am seeking.

Use **UNINTERESTED** to mean 'bored'.

His teachers say he is reluctant to participate and is clearly **UNINTERESTED** in any activities the school has to offer.

Originally, **DISINTERESTED** was used in this sense (= having no interest in, apathetic), and it is interesting that this meaning is being revived in popular speech.

→

Avoid this use in formal contexts, however, for it is widely perceived as being incorrect.

disiple

Wrong spelling. See DISCIPLE.

disk

See DISC OR DISK?.

displace or misplace?

To displace is to move someone or something from its usual place:

a **DISPLACED** hip; a **DISPLACED** person

To misplace something is to put it in the wrong place (and possibly forget where it is):

a **MISPLACED** apostrophe; **MISPLACED** kindness

dissappear

Wrong spelling. See DISAPPEAR.

dissappoint

Wrong spelling. See DISAPPOINT.

dissapprove

Wrong spelling. See DISAPPROVE.

dissatisfied

(dis + satisfied)

dissociate

See DISASSOCIATE OR DISSOCIATE?.

distroy

Wrong spelling. See DESTROY.

divers or diverse

The first is rarely used nowadays except jokingly or in mistake for the second.

DIVERS means 'several', 'of varying types': **DIVERS** reference books.

DIVERSE means 'very different': **DIVERSE** opinions,

DIVERSE interests.

does or dose?

DOES he take sugar? He **DOES**. (pronounced 'duz')
Take a **DOSE** of cough mixture every three hours.

doesn't

(*not* does'nt)
See CONTRACTIONS.

domino (singular) dominoes (plural)

See PLURALS (iv).

don't

(*not* do'nt)
See CONTRACTIONS.

dose

See DOES OR DOSE?.

double meaning

See AMBIGUITY.

double negatives

The effect of two negatives is to cancel each other
out. This is sometimes done deliberately and can be
effective:

I am not ungenerous. (= I am very generous.)
He is not unintelligent. (= He is quite intelligent.)

Frequently, however, it is not intentional and the
writer ends up saying the opposite of what is meant:

I haven't had no tea. (= I have had tea.)
You don't know nothing. (= You know something.)

Be particularly careful with 'barely', 'scarcely',
'hardly'. These have a negative force.

I wasn't **SCARCELY** awake when you rang. (= I
was very awake.)

Be careful too with constructions like this:

→

I wouldn't be surprised if he didn't come.

Say either: I wouldn't be surprised if he
came.
or: I would be surprised if he
didn't come.

Sometimes writers put so many negatives in a
sentence that the meaning becomes too complicated
to unravel:

Mr Brown denied vehemently that it was unlikely
that no one would come to the concert.

Does Mr Brown think that the concert will be
popular or not?

Rewrite as either:

Mr Brown was certain the concert would be well
attended.
Or: Mr Brown feared that no one would come to the
concert.

doubling rule
See **ADDING ENDINGS** (i) and (iv).

doubt
(*not* dout)
The word is derived from the Latin word *dubitare*,
to doubt. It may help you to remember that the
silent b is there.

Down's Syndrome
(*not* Downe's)

downstairs
(one word)

draft or draught?
A **DRAFT** is a first or subsequent attempt at a piece
of written work before it is finished.
A **DRAUGHT** is a current of cool air in a room.

One also refers to a **DRAUGHT** of ale, a game of
DRAUGHTS and a boat having a shallow **DRAUGHT**.

drawers or draws?
DRAWS is a verb.

She **DRAWS** very well for a young child.

DRAWERS is a noun.

The **DRAWERS** of the sideboard are very stiff.

dreamed/dreamt
Both spellings are correct.

drier or dryer?
DRIER is generally used for the comparative form
(**DRIER** = more dry).
DRYER is generally used for a drying machine (hair
DRYER, clothes **DRYER**).
However, both spellings are interchangeable.

drunkenness
drunken + ness

dryness
(exception to the -y rule)
See ADDING ENDINGS (iii).

dual or duel?
DUAL means two (e.g. **DUAL** controls, **DUAL**
carriageway).
DUEL means fight or contest.

duchess
(*not* dutchess)

due to/owing to
Strictly speaking, 'due to' should refer to a noun:

His *absence* was **DUE TO** sickness. (noun)
The *delay* was **DUE TO** leaves on the line. (noun)

'Owing to', strictly speaking, should refer to a verb: ➝

The march *was cancelled* **OWING TO** the storm.
(verb)
OWING TO an earlier injury, he *limped* badly.
(verb)

However, in recent years, the use of 'due to' where traditionally 'owing to' would be required has become widespread. Nevertheless, some careful writers continue to preserve the distinction and you may wish to do so too in a formal context.

duel
> See DUAL OR DUEL?.

duly
> (*not* duely)
> This is an exception to the magic -e rule.
> See ADDING ENDINGS (ii).

dutchess
> Wrong spelling. See DUCHESS.

dwelled/dwelt
> Both spellings are correct.

dyeing or dying?
> **DYEING** comes from the verb to dye.
> She was **DYEING** all her vests green.
> **DYING** comes from the verb to die.
> She cursed him with her **DYING** breath.

earnest or Ernest?
> **EARNEST** = serious and sincere
> **ERNEST** = masculine first name

echo (singular) echoes (plural)
> See PLURALS (iv).

economic or economical?
> **ECONOMIC** = related to the economy of the country, or industry or business
> **ECONOMICAL** = thrifty, avoiding extravagance

ecstasy (singular) ecstasies (plural)
> See PLURALS (iv).

Ecstasy
> illegal drug

eczema

-ed or -t?
> These can be either:

burned	burnt
dreamed	dreamt
dwelled	dwelt
kneeled	knelt
leaned	leant
leaped	leapt
learned	learnt
smelled	smelt
spelled	spelt
spilled	spilt
spoiled	spoilt

eerie or eyrie?
> **EERIE** = strange, weird, disturbing
> **EYRIE** = an eagle's nest

effect

See AFFECT OR EFFECT?.

effective, effectual or efficient?

EFFECTIVE = able to produce a result:

an **EFFECTIVE** cure
an **EFFECTIVE** speech

EFFECTUAL = likely to be completely successful:

EFFECTUAL prayer
EFFECTUAL legislation

EFFICIENT = working well without wasting time, money or effort:

an **EFFICIENT** secretary
an **EFFICIENT** engine

ei/ie spelling rule

Remember the jingle:

i before **e**
except after **c**
or when sounded like **a**
as in 'neighbour' and 'weigh'.

Here are some examples which follow the rule. There are plenty of others.

ie	*ei after c*
achieve	ceiling
believe	conceited
chief	conceive
field	perceive
friend	receive
hygiene	*ei sounding like a*
priest	eight
relief	reign
retrieve	reindeer
shield	skein
shriek	sleigh
thief	vein

18 exceptions

caffeine	forfeit	seize
codeine	heifer	sheikh
counterfeit	height	sovereign
either	leisure	surfeit
Fahrenheit	neither	weir
foreign	protein	weird

Proper names (e.g. of people or countries) don't follow the rule: Deirdre, Keith, Neil, Sheila, Madeira, etc.

eighth

(*notice* -hth)
See EI/IE SPELLING RULE.

either

(*not* -ie-) An exception to the EI/IE SPELLING RULE.

either...or

(i) Take care with singular and plural verbs.
Use these exemplar sentences as a guide:

Either Jack or Tom *was* there. (singular verb to match Jack (singular) or Tom (singular))

Either Jack or his brothers *were* there. (plural verb to match 'brothers' (plural) which is closer to it than 'Jack' (singular))

Either his brothers or Jack *was* there. (singular verb this time because 'Jack' (singular) is closer to the verb than 'brothers')

(ii) Be careful to place each part of the 'either...or' construction correctly.

✗ I have decided either that I have to build an extension or I have to move.

✓ I have decided that either I have to build an extension or I have to move.

→

In the example above, there are these two possibilities:

I have to build an extension.
I have to move.

'Either' precedes the first one and 'or' precedes the second.

The second one could be shortened:

I have decided that either I have to build an extension or (I have to) move.
✓ I have decided that either I have to build an extension or move.

It is important that the two constructions following 'either' and 'or' should be parallel ones:

either meat or fish
either green or red
either to love or to hate
either with malice or with kindness.

If the second construction is shortened to avoid repetition, this is fine. The missing words are obvious and can be supplied readily.

elf (singular) elves (plural)
See PLURALS (v).

eligible or legible?
  ELIGIBLE = suitably qualified
  LEGIBLE = able to be read

eloquent

elude
  See ALLUDE OR ELUDE?.

embargo (singular) embargoes (plural)
  See PLURALS (iv).

embarrass
embarrassed, embarrassing (*not* -r-)

embarrassment

emend
See AMEND OR EMEND?.

emergency (singular) emergencies (plural)
See PLURALS (iv).

emigrant or immigrant?
An **EMIGRANT** leaves his or her country to live in another.
An **IMMIGRANT** moves into a country to live permanently.

eminent or imminent?
EMINENT = famous
IMMINENT = about to happen

emperor

emphasise/emphasize
Both spellings are correct.

encyclopaedia/encyclopedia
Both spellings are correct.

endeavour

end stops
There are three end stops: a full stop (.), an exclamation mark (!), and a question mark (?).

Use a full stop to end a statement.

There are five eggs in the fridge.

Use an exclamation mark with a command or an exclamation.

Get out!

Use a question mark to end a question.

→

Where do you live?

See EXCLAMATION MARKS.
   FULL STOPS.
   QUESTION MARKS.

endings
See ADDING ENDINGS.

enemy (singular) enemies (plural)
See PLURALS (iv).

enormity
This refers to a grave sin or a crime, or a disaster on a huge scale.

We gradually realised the full **ENORMITY** of the tragedy.

It is often used in popular speech to mean 'enormousness', 'hugeness', 'immensity'. This should be avoided in a formal context.

enquiry or inquiry?
Both spellings are correct and there is no difference in meaning. British English favours the first and American English the second.

Some writers reserve the first for a general request for information and the second for a formal investigation, but this is by no means necessary.

enrol
enrolled, enrolling
(British English – enrol; American English – enroll)

enrolment
(British English – enrolment; American English – enrollment)

ensure or insure?
to **ENSURE** = to make sure
to **INSURE** = to arrange for financial compensation in the case of loss, injury, damage or death

enthusiasm
   (*not* -ou-)

enthusiastic

envelop
   enveloped, enveloping, envelopment (stress on
   second syllable)

envelope (singular)
   envelopes (plural) (stress on third syllable)

environment
   (*not* enviroment)

epigram or epitaph?
   EPIGRAM = a short witty saying
   EPITAPH = an inscription on a tombstone

equip
   equipped, equipping, equipment
   See ADDING ENDINGS (iv).

Ernest
   See EARNEST OR ERNEST?.

erratum (singular) errata (plural)
   See FOREIGN PLURALS.

erring
   err + ing (*not* -r-)

erupt
   (*not* -rr-)

especially or specially?
   The two words are very close in meaning and
   sometimes overlap. However, use these exemplar
   sentences as a guide to exclusive uses:

   I bought the car **ESPECIALLY** for you (= for you
   alone).
   We are awaiting a **SPECIALLY** commissioned report
   (= for a special purpose).

estuary (singular) estuaries (plural)
See PLURALS (iv).

etc.
(*not* e.t.c. or ect.)

(i) etc. is an abbreviation of the Latin *et cetera* which means 'and other things'. It is therefore incorrect to write 'and etc.'.

(ii) Avoid using 'etc.' in formal writing. Either list all the items indicated by the vague and lazy 'etc.', or introduce the given selection with a phrase like 'including', 'such as' or 'for example'.

eventually
eventual + ly (*not* eventully)

exaggerate
(*not* exagerate)

examination

exausted
Wrong spelling. See EXHAUSTED.

excellent
(*not* -ant)

except
See ACCEPT OR EXCEPT?.

exceptionable or exceptional?
EXCEPTIONABLE = open to objection
EXCEPTIONAL = unusual

excercise
Wrong spelling. See EXERCISE.

excite
excited, exciting, excitement
See ADDING ENDINGS (ii).

exclaim
exclaimed, exclaiming

exclamation
(*not* -claim-)

exclamation mark
Use an exclamation mark:

(i) with exclamations
     Ouch! Oh! Hey!

(ii) with vehement commands
     Stop thief! Help! Jump!

     See COMMANDS.

exercise
(*not* excercise)

exhausted
(*not* exausted)

exhausting or exhaustive?
EXHAUSTING = tiring
EXHAUSTIVE = thorough, fully comprehensive

exhibition

exhilarated
(not -er-)

expedition
(*not* expidition)
The second syllable is derived from the Latin word
pes, *pedis* (foot, of the foot). This may help you to
remember -ped-. The words pedal, pedestrian,
pedometer all come from this same Latin root.

expendable
(*not* -ible)

expense

expensive

experience
(*not* expierience, *not* -ance)
The second syllable is derived from the Latin word *per*, meaning through. (Experience is what we gain from going 'through' something.)

explain
explained, explaining

explanation
(*not* -plain-)

explicit or implicit?
EXPLICIT = stated clearly and openly
IMPLICIT = implied but not actually stated

exspense
Wrong spelling. See EXPENSE.

exspensive
Wrong spelling. See EXPENSIVE.

exstremely
Wrong spelling. See EXTREMELY.

extraordinary
extra + ordinary

extravagance
(*not* -ence)

extravagant
(*not* -ent)

extremely
extreme + ly

extrordinary
Wrong spelling. See EXTRAORDINARY.

exuberance
(*not* -ence)

exuberant

(*not* -ent)

eyrie

See **EERIE OR EYRIE?**.

facetious

(All five vowels occur in this word once only and in alphabetical order.)

facilities or faculties?
FACILITIES = amenities
FACULTIES = mental or physical aptitudes

facinate

Wrong spelling. See FASCINATE.

factory (singular) factories (plural)
See PLURALS (iv).

Fahrenheit

(*not* -ie-)
See EI/IE SPELLING RULE.

faithfully

faithful + ly
See SINCERELY for guidelines when punctuating a complimentary close to a letter (fully blocked and also traditional layout).

familiar

(*not* fammiliar)

family (singular) families (plural)
(*not* -mm-)

farther or further?

Both words can be used to refer to physical distance although some writers prefer to keep 'farther' for this purpose.

I can walk **FARTHER** than you.
I can walk **FURTHER** than you.

FURTHER is used in a figurative sense:

Nothing was **FURTHER** from my mind.

FURTHER is also used in certain expressions:

FURTHER education
until **FURTHER** notice

fascinate
(*not* facinate)

favourite
(*not* -ate)

feasible
(*not* -able)

February
Notice the word has four syllables and not three as it is often mispronounced.

fewer or less?
FEWER is the comparative form of 'few'.
It is used with plural nouns:

FEWER vegetables
FEWER responsibilities
FEWER children

LESS is the comparative form of 'little'.
It is used in the sense of 'a small amount' rather than 'a fewer number of':

LESS enthusiasm
LESS sugar
LESS petrol

LESS THAN is used with number alone, and expressions of time and distance:

LESS THAN a thousand
LESS THAN ten seconds
LESS THAN four miles

It is considered incorrect to use 'less' instead of 'fewer' although such confusion is frequent in popular speech.

As a rule of thumb, remember:

FEWER = not so many
LESS = not so much

fiancé or fiancée?
FIANCÉ = masculine
FIANCÉE = feminine
Note the accent in both words.

fictional or fictitious?
FICTIONAL = invented for the purpose of fiction, related to fiction

FICTIONAL texts
FICTIONAL writing

FICTITIOUS = false, not true

a **FICTITIOUS** report
a **FICTITIOUS** name and address

Either word can be used to describe a character in a work of fiction: a **FICTIONAL** or **FICTITIOUS** character.

fiery
(*not* firey)

fifteen
fifteenth

fifth

fifty
fiftieth

finally
final + ly (*not* -aly)

finish

finished, finishing (*not* -nn-)

firey

Wrong spelling. See FIERY.

flamingo (singular) flamingoes or flamingos (plural)

flammable or inflammable

Both words mean 'easily bursting into flame'. People often think that inflammable is the negative form but the prefix 'in' here means 'into'.

The opposite of these two words is non-flammable or non-inflammable.

flaunt or flout?

FLAUNT = to show off. **FLAUNT** one's wealth.
FLOUT = to disregard. **FLOUT** all the rules.

flee

they fled, have fled, are fleeing

flexible

(*not* -able)

flu or flue?

FLU = influenza (*not* 'flu although an abbreviation)
FLUE = a pipe or duct for smoke and gases

fluorescent

(*not* flourescent)

fly

they flew, have flown, are flying

focus

focused or focussed (both correct)
focusing or focussing (both correct)

for- or fore-?

A useful rule of thumb is to remember the usual meaning of the prefixes:

→

FOR- = not, or something negative
(forbid, forfeit, forget, forsake)
FORE- = before
(foreboding, forecast, forefathers)
See individual entries for
FORBEAR OR FOREBEAR?
FOREWORD OR FORWARD?.

forbear or forebear?

FORBEAR (stress on second syllable) = restrain
oneself
FORBEAR or **FOREBEAR** (stress on first syllable)
= ancestor

forbid

forbad or forbade (both correct), forbidden,
forbidding

forcible

(*not* -able)

forecast

(*not* forcast)

forefend/forfend

Either spelling can be used.

foregather/forgather

Either spelling can be used.

forego/forgo

Either spelling can be used.

foreign

An exception to the rule.
See **EI/IE SPELLING RULE**.

foreign plurals

Some foreign words in English have retained their
foreign plurals. Some have both foreign and English
plurals. Take care, however, with the words that are
asterisked because the foreign plural of these is used

in a different sense from the English plural. Check these words under individual entries for the distinction in meaning.

singular -a	foreign plural	English plural
alga	algae	–
antenna	antennae*	antennas*
formula	formulae*	formulas*
larva	larvae	–
nebula	nebulae	nebulas
vertebra	vertebrae	vertebras

singular -eau -eu	foreign plural	English plural
adieu	adieux	adieus
bureau	bureaux	bureaus
chateau	chateaux	–
milieu	milieux	milieus
plateau	plateaux	plateaus
tableau	tableaux	–

singular -ex -ix		
appendix	appendices*	appendixes*
index	indices*	indexes*
matrix	matrices	matrixes
vortex	vortices	vortexes

singular -is		
analysis	analyses	–
axis	axes	–
crisis	crises	–
diagnosis	diagnoses	–
hypothesis	hypotheses	–
parenthesis	parentheses	–
synopsis	synopses	–

singular -o		
graffito	graffiti	–
libretto	libretti	librettos
tempo	tempi	tempos
virtuoso	virtuosi	virtuosos

→

singular -on	foreign plural	English plural
automaton	automata	automatons
criterion	criteria	–
ganglion	ganglia	ganglions
phenomenon	phenomena	–

singular -um		
aquarium	aquaria	aquariums
bacterium	bacteria	–
curriculum	curricula	curriculums
datum	data	–
erratum	errata	–
memorandum	memoranda	memorandums
millennium	millennia	millenniums
referendum	referenda	referendums
stratum	strata	–
ultimatum	ultimata	ultimatums

singular -um		
ovum	ova	–

singular -us		
bacillus	bacilli	–
cactus	cacti	cactuses
fungus	fungi	funguses
hippopotamus	hippopotami	hippopotamuses
nucleus	nuclei	–
radius	radii	radiuses
stimulus	stimuli	–
syllabus	syllabi	syllabuses
terminus	termini	terminuses
tumulus	tumuli	–

The Hebrew plural -im is found in these three words:

cherub	cherubim	cherubs
kibbutz	kibbutzim	–
seraph	seraphim	–

This list is by no means comprehensive but it does contain most of the words that are commonly used.

foresake

Wrong spelling. See FORSAKE.

forest

(*not* forrest)

foreword or forward?

Use these exemplar sentences as a guide:

The Poet Laureate had written a **FOREWORD** for the new anthology.
I am looking **FORWARD** to the holiday.
Will you please **FORWARD** this letter?

forfeit

(*not* -ie-, exception to the rule)
See EI/IE SPELLING RULE.

forfend

See FOREFEND/FORFEND.

forgather

See FOREGATHER/FORGATHER.

forgo

See FOREGO/FORGO.

formally or formerly?

FORMALLY = in a formal manner
FORMERLY = previously, at an earlier time

formula (singular)

There are two plurals.
Use formulae in a scientific or mathematical context.
Use formulas in all other cases.

forrest

Wrong spelling. See FOREST.

forsake

(*not* fore-)
See FOR OR FORE?.

fortunately

fortunate + ly (*not* -atly)
See ADDING ENDINGS (ii).

forty
(*not* fourty)

forward
See FOREWORD OR FORWARD?.

frantic

frantically
frantic + ally (*not* franticly)

freind
Wrong spelling. See FRIEND.

frequent
(*not* -ant)
Use as an adjective (stress on first syllable):

There were **FREQUENT** interruptions.

Use as a verb (stress on second syllable):

They **FREQUENT** the most terrible pubs.

fresco (singular) frescoes or frescos (plural)

friend
(*not* -ei-)

frieze
(*not* -ei-)
See EI/IE SPELLING RULE.

frighten
frightened, frightening
(*not* frightend, frightning)

frolic
frolicked, frolicking, frolicsome
See SOFT C AND SOFT G.

fuchsia
(named after Leonhard Fuchs, German botanist)

-ful

When full is used as an ending to a word, it is always spelt -ful:

beautiful
careful
wonderful
hopeful, etc.

fulfil

fulfilled, fulfilling, fulfilment
See ADDING ENDINGS (iv).

full stops

See END STOPS.
See COMMAS (b).

fungus (singular) fungi or funguses (plural)
See FOREIGN PLURALS.

further

See FARTHER OR FURTHER?.

fuschia

Wrong spelling. See FUCHSIA.

gaiety

gay + ety – an exception to the y rule
See ADDING ENDINGS (iii).

gaily

gay + ly – an exception to the y rule
See ADDING ENDINGS (iii).

gallop

galloped, galloping (*not* -pp-)
See ADDING ENDINGS (iv).

ganglion (singular) ganglia or ganglions (plural)
See FOREIGN PLURALS.

gaol

An alternative spelling is 'jail'.

garage

gastly

Wrong spelling. See GHASTLY.

gateau (singular) gateaus or gateaux (plural)
See FOREIGN PLURALS.

gauge

(*not* guage)

genealogical

(*not* geneo-)

generosity

(*not* -ous-)

generous

get

they get, have got, are getting

ghastly
>(*not* gastly)

gipsy/gypsy
>Both spellings are correct.
>gipsies or gypsies (plural)
>See PLURALS (iii).

glamorous
>(*not* -our-)

glamour

good will or goodwill?
>Always write as one word when referring to the prestige and trading value of a business.

>He bought the **GOODWILL** for five thousand pounds.

>Use either two words or one word when referring to general feelings of kindness and support.

>As a gesture of **GOOD WILL**, she cancelled the fine.

gorgeous
>(*not* -gous)
>See SOFT C AND SOFT G.

gorilla or guerilla?
>A **GORILLA** is an animal.
>A **GUERILLA** is a revolutionary fighter.

gossip
>gossiped, gossiping (*not* -pp)
>See ADDING ENDINGS (iv).

gourmand or gourmet?
>A **GOURMAND** is greedy and over-indulges where fine food is concerned.
>A **GOURMET** is a connoisseur of fine food.

government
   (*not* goverment as it is often mispronounced)

governor
   (*not* -er)

gradual

gradually
   gradual + ly (*not* gradully)

graffiti
   This is increasingly used in a general sense (like the word 'writing') and its plural force is forgotten when it comes to matching it with a verb:

   There *was* **GRAFFITI** all over the wall.

   A few conservative writers would like a plural verb. (There were **GRAFFITI** all over the wall.)

graffito (singular) graffiti (plural)
   See FOREIGN PLURALS.

grammar
   (*not* -er)

gramophone
   (*not* grama-)

grandad/granddad
   Both spellings are correct.

grandchild

granddaughter

grandfather

grandma

grandmother

grandparent

grandson

grate or great?

Use these exemplar sentences as a guide:

The fire was burning brightly in the **GRATE**.
GRATE the potato coarsely.
Christopher Wren was a **GREAT** architect.

grateful

(*not* greatful)

grief

(*not* -ei-)

grievance

(*not* -ence)

grievous

(*not* -ious)

grotto (singular)

grottoes or grottos (plural)

guage

Wrong spelling. See GAUGE.

guarantee

guardian

guess

guest

guttural

(*not* -er-)

H

hadn't
(*not* had'nt)

haemorrhage
(*not* -rh-)

half (singular) halves (plural)
See PLURALS (v).

halo (singular) haloes or halos (plural)
See PLURALS (iv).

handkerchief (singular) handkerchiefs (plural) (*not* -nk-)
See PLURALS (v).

hanged or hung?
People are **HANGED**.
Things like clothes and pictures are **HUNG**.

happen
happened, happening (*not* -nn-)

harass
(*not* -rr-)

hardly
See DOUBLE NEGATIVES.

hasn't
(*not* has'nt)

haven't
(*not* have'nt)

headquarters
(*not* headquaters)

hear or here?
You **HEAR** with your ear.

Use **HERE** to indicate place:

Come over **HERE**.

heard or herd?
We **HEARD** their voices outside.
We photographed the **HERD** of deer.

heifer
See EI/IE SPELLING RULE.

height
See EI/IE SPELLING RULE.

heinous
See EI/IE SPELLING RULE.

herd
See HEARD OR HERD?.

here
See HEAR OR HERE?.

hero (singular) heroes (plural)
See PLURALS (iv).

heroin or heroine?
HEROIN is a drug.
A **HEROINE** is a female hero.

hers
No apostrophe is needed.

This is mine; this is **HERS**.
HERS has a yellow handle.

hiccough or hiccup?
Both words are pronounced 'hiccup' and either
spelling can be used. The second spelling (hiccup) is
more usual.

hiccup
hiccuped, hiccuping (*not* -pp-)

hieroglyphics

high-tech or hi-tec?

Both spellings are correct for the adjective derived from high technology:

A **HI-TEC** factory
A **HIGH-TECH** computer system

Without the hyphen, each word can be used as a noun replacing 'high technology':

A generation familiar with **HIGH TECH**
The latest development in **HI TEC**

hindrance

(*not* hinderance)

hippopotamus (singular) hippopotami or hippopotamuses (plural)

See FOREIGN PLURALS.

historic or historical?

HISTORIC means famous in history, memorable, or likely to go down in recorded history:

a **HISTORIC** meeting

HISTORICAL means existing in the past or representing something that could have happened in the past:

a **HISTORICAL** novel
a **HISTORICAL** fact

Note It would not be wrong to say or write *an* historic meeting, *an* historical novel, *an* historical fact. However, this usage of *an* before words like hotel, historic and historical is becoming much less common, now that the h beginning these words is usually voiced.

hoard or horde?

To **HOARD** is to save something in a secret place.
A **HOARD** is a secret store.

A **HORDE** is a large group of people, insects or animals.

hoarse or horse?

HOARSE means croaky, sore or rough (a **HOARSE** whisper).
HORSE is an animal.

hole or whole?

Use these exemplar sentences as a guide:

She ate the **WHOLE** cake by herself.
You have a **HOLE** in your sock.

homeoepathy/homeopathy

Both spellings are correct.

honest

(*not* onnist or honist)

honorary

(*Note*: this word has four syllables not three.)
An **HONORARY** secretary of an association is one who works voluntarily and receives no payment.

honour

honourable

hoof (singular) hoofs or hooves (plural)

See PLURALS (v).

hoping or hopping?

hope + ing = hoping
hop + ing = hopping
See ADDING ENDINGS (i) and (ii).

horde

See HOARD OR HORDE?.

horrible

(*not* -able)

horse

See HOARSE OR HORSE?.

human or humane?

HUMAN beings are naturally competitive.
There must be a more **HUMANE** way of slaughtering animals.

humour

humorous (*not* humourous)
humourless

hundred

(*not* hundered)

hung

See HANGED OR HUNG?.

hygiene

(*not* -ei-)
See EI/IE SPELLING RULE.

hyper- or hypo-?

The prefix 'hyper' comes from a Greek word meaning 'over', 'beyond'. Hence we have words like these:

hyperactive   (= abnormally active)
hypermarket   (= a very large self-service store)
hypersensitive (= unusually sensitive)

The prefix 'hypo' comes from a Greek word meaning 'under'. Hence we have words like these:

hypochondria (the melancholy associated with obsession with one's health was originally believed to originate in the organs beneath the ribs)
hypodermic (= under the skin)

hypercritical or hypocritical?

HYPERCRITICAL = excessively critical

HYPOCRITICAL = disguising one's true nature under a pretence of being better than one really is
See HYPER- OR HYPO-?.

hyperthermia or hypothermia?
HYPERTHERMIA = having an abnormally high body temperature
HYPOTHERMIA = having an abnormally low body temperature
See HYPER- OR HYPO-?.

hyperventilate or hypoventilate
HYPERVENTILATE = to breathe at an abnormally rapid rate
HYPOVENTILATE = to breathe at an abnormally slow rate
See HYPER- OR HYPO-?.

hyphens
(i) Hyphens are used to indicate word-breaks where there is not space to complete a word at the end of a line.

Take care to divide the word at an appropriate point between syllables so that your reader is not confused and can continue smoothly from the first part of the word to the second part.

There are dictionaries of hyphenation available that will indicate sensible places to break words. They don't always agree with each other! You will also notice a difference in practice between British English and American English.

Increasingly, however, the trend is towards American English practice, i.e. being guided by the way the word is pronounced. Break the word in such a way as to preserve the overall pronunciation as far as possible. It is really a matter of common sense. For this reason you will avoid breaking:

→

father	into	fat-her
legend	into	leg-end
therapist	into	the-rapist
manslaughter	into	mans-laughter
notable	into	not-able
		and so on!

Note: that the hyphen should be placed at the end of the first line (to indicate that the word is to be continued). It is not repeated at the beginning of the next.

The children shouted enthusias-
tically as they raced towards the sea.

If you are breaking a word that is already hyphenated, break it at the existing hyphen:

Both my parents are extremely absent-
minded.

Breaking a word always makes it look temporarily unfamiliar. You will notice that in printed books for very young readers word-breaks are always carefully avoided. Ideally, you also will try to avoid them. Anticipate how much space a word requires at the end of a line and start a new line if necessary. Whatever happens, avoid breaking a word very close to its beginning or its end, and never break a one-syllabled word.

(ii) Hyphens are used to join compound numbers between 21 and 99:

twenty-one	twenty-five
fifty-five	fifty-fifth
ninety-nine	ninety-ninth

Hyphens are also used to join fractions when they are written as words:

three-quarters
five-ninths

(iii) Hyphens are used to join compound words so that they become one word:

my son-in-law
a twenty-pound note
her happy-go-lucky smile

You will sometimes need to check in a dictionary whether a word is hyphenated or not. Sometimes words written separately in a ten-year-old dictionary will be hyphenated in a more modern one; sometimes words hyphenated in an older dictionary will now be written as one word.
    Is it washing machine or washing-machine, wash-basin or washbasin, print-out or printout?
    Such words need to be checked individually.

(iv) Hyphens are used with some prefixes:

co-author, ex-wife, anti-censorship

Check individual words in a dictionary if you are in doubt.
    Always use a hyphen when you are using a prefix before a word that begins with a capital letter:

pro-British, anti-Christian, un-American

Sometimes a hyphen is used for the sake of clarity. There is a difference in meaning between the words in these pairs:

re-cover and recover
re-form and reform
co-respondent and correspondent

(v) Hyphens are also used to indicate a range of figures or dates:

→

There were 12 - 20 people in the room.
He was killed in the 1914 - 18 war.

hypocrisy
(*not* -asy)

hypocrite

hypocritical
See **HYPERCRITICAL OR HYPOCRITICAL?**.

hypothermia
See **HYPERTHERMIA OR HYPOTHERMIA?**.

hypothesis (singular) hypotheses (plural)
See **FOREIGN PLURALS**.

hypoventilate
See **HYPERVENTILATE OR HYPOVENTILATE?**.

I/me/myself

These three words are pronouns and cause a great deal of confusion.

(i) Most people use the pronoun 'I' correctly when it is used on its own:

I love cats.
I like chocolate.
I mow the lawn every Sunday.
I am trying to lose weight.
I have two sisters.

Confusion generally arises with phrases like 'my husband and I' and 'my husband and me'. Which should it be?

The simplest method is to break the sentence into two and see whether 'I' or 'me' sounds right:

My husband likes chocolate.
I like chocolate.
MY HUSBAND AND I like chocolate.

(ii) Most people use the pronoun 'me' correctly when it is used on its own:

The burglar threatened **ME**.
It was given to **ME**.

Once again confusion arises when a pair is involved. The advice remains the same. Break the sentence into two and see whether 'I' or 'me' sounds right:

The burglar threatened my husband.
The burglar threatened **ME**.
The burglar threatened **MY HUSBAND AND ME**.

It was given to my husband.

$\rightarrow$

It was given to **ME**.
It was given to **MY HUSBAND AND ME**.

(iii) The pronoun 'myself' has two distinct functions.

♦   It can be used in constructions like this where it is essential to the sense:

I cut **MYSELF** yesterday.
I did it by **MYSELF**.

♦   It can be used to help emphasise a point. In these cases, it can be omitted without changing the overall sense:

I'll wrap the parcel **MYSELF**.
MYSELF, I would disagree.

'Myself' should never be used as a substitute for 'I' or 'me'.

✗   My friend and myself had a wonderful time in Austria.
✓   My friend and I had a wonderful time.

✗   They presented my brother and myself with a silver cup.
✓   They presented my brother and me with a silver cup.

✗   This is from Henry and myself.
✓   This is from Henry and me.

-ible

See **-ABLE/-IBLE**.

idea or ideal?

Bristolians have particular difficulty distinguishing between these two because of the intrusive Bristol 'l'. These exemplar sentences should help:

Your **IDEA** is brilliant.
This is an **IDEAL** spot for a picnic.
His **IDEALS** prevent him from eating meat.

idiosyncrasy
(*not* -cy)

-ie-
See EI/IE SPELLING RULE.

illegible or ineligible?
ILLEGIBLE = not able to be read
INELIGIBLE = not properly qualified

illusion
See ALLUSION, DELUSION OR ILLUSION?.

imaginary or imaginative?
IMAGINARY = existing only in the imagination
IMAGINATIVE = showing or having a vivid
imagination, being creative, original

imformation
Wrong spelling. See INFORMATION.

immediately
(*not* immeadiately or immediatly)

immense
immensely (*not* immensly)

immigrant
See EMIGRANT OR IMMIGRANT?.

imminent
See EMINENT, OR IMMINENT?.

immoral
See AMORAL OR IMMORAL?.

implicit
See EXPLICIT OR IMPLICIT?.

imply or infer?
To **IMPLY** something is to hint at it:

She **IMPLIED** that there were strong moral objections
to his appointment but didn't say so in so many words.

→

To **INFER** is to draw a conclusion:

Am I to **INFER** from what you say that he is unsuitable for the post?

impossible
(*not* -able)

imposter/impostor
Both spellings are correct. The second form (-or) is, however, more common.

impractical or impracticable?
IMPRACTICAL = could be done but not worth doing
IMPRACTICABLE = incapable of being done

incidentally
incidental + ly (*not* incidently)

incredible
(*not* -able)

indefensible
(*not* -able)

indelible
(*not* -able)

independence
(*not* -ance)

independent
(*not* -ant)

index (singular) indexes or indices (plural)
See FOREIGN PLURALS.
See INDEXES OR INDICES?.

indexes or indices?
Both are acceptable plural forms of 'index' but they are used differently.
Use **INDEXES** to refer to alphabetical lists of references in books.

Use **INDICES** in mathematical, economic and technical contexts.

indirect speech/reported speech

Unlike direct speech where the words actually spoken are enclosed within inverted commas, indirect speech requires no inverted commas.

Direct: 'I am exhausted,' said Sheila.
Indirect: Sheila said that she was exhausted.

Note how direct questions and commands become straightforward statements when they are reported in indirect speech. A full stop at the end is sufficient.

Direct: 'What is your name?' Mr Brown asked the new boy.
Indirect: Mr Brown asked the new boy his name.

Direct: 'Fire!' commanded the officer.
Indirect: The officer commanded his men to fire.

indispensable

(*not* -ible)

individual

(five syllables)

This noun should correctly be used to distinguish one person from the rest of a group or community:

the rights of the **INDIVIDUAL** in society

Informally it is also used in the sense of 'person':

an untrustworthy **INDIVIDUAL**

Avoid this use in formal contexts.

industrial or industrious?

INDUSTRIAL = associated with manufacturing
INDUSTRIOUS = hard-working

ineffective or ineffectual?

INEFFECTIVE = not producing the desired effect

→

an **INEFFECTIVE** speech

INEFFECTUAL = not capable of producing the desired effect

an **INEFFECTUAL** speaker

ineligible
See ILLEGIBLE OR INELIGIBLE?.

inexhaustible

in fact
(two words)

infectious
See CONTAGIOUS OR INFECTIOUS?.

infer
See IMPLY OR INFER?. See also next entry.

infer
inferred, inferring, inference
See ADDING ENDINGS (iv).

inflammable
See FLAMMABLE OR INFLAMMABLE?.
See also next entry.

inflammable or inflammatory?
INFLAMMABLE = easily bursting into flames
INFLAMMATORY = tending to arouse violent feelings

information
(*not* im-)

in front
two words (*not* frount)

ingenious or ingenuous?
INGENIOUS = skilful, inventive, original
INGENUOUS = innocent, unsophisticated

inhuman or inhumane?
INHUMAN = lacking all human qualities
INHUMANE = lacking compassion and kindness

innocent
innocence

innocuous

innuendo (singular) innuendoes or innuendos (plural)
See PLURALS (iv).

inoculate
(*not* -nn-)

inquiry
See ENQUIRY OR INQUIRY?.

instal/install
Both spellings are correct.
installed, installing, installment/instalment

insurance
See ASSURANCE OR INSURANCE?.

intelligence
(*not* -ance)

intelligent
(*not* -ant)

intentions
(*not* intensions)

inter-/intra-
The prefix **INTER-** means between or among (e.g. international).
The prefix **INTRA-** means within, on the inside (e.g. intravenous).

interesting
(four syllables, *not* intresting)

interrogate

(not -r-)

interrupt

(not -r-)

invent

See DISCOVER OR INVENT?.

inverted commas

Inverted commas can be double (" ") or single (' '). Use whichever you wish as long as you are consistent. In print, single inverted commas are generally used; in handwriting, double inverted commas are frequently used for enclosing direct speech and single inverted commas for enclosing titles and quotations. There are no hard-and-fast rules.

Direct speech
Inverted commas should enclose the actual words of speech that are being quoted.

'You are very welcome,' she said.
She said, 'You are very welcome.'
'You are,' she said, 'very welcome.'

Note the punctuation conventions in the sentences above. These will be examined more closely now.

◆   Speech first and narrative second.

'You are very welcome,' she said.
'Are you tired?' she asked.
'Not at all!' he exclaimed.

Notice that the appropriate punctuation is enclosed with the words spoken.

Note that the narrative continues with an initial small letter: she/he.

◆ Narrative first and speech second.

> Brian said, 'You're very late.'
> Brian asked, 'What kept you?'
> Sarah snapped, 'Don't cross-question me!'

Notice that a comma always divides the narrative from the direct speech.

Note that the direct speech always begins with a capital letter.

Note that the appropriate punctuation mark is enclosed within the inverted commas with the words spoken and no further end stop is required.

◆ Speech interrupted by narrative.

> 'We have all been hoping,' said my mother, 'that you will join us on Christmas Day.'

Note that the two parts of the interrupted spoken sentence are enclosed by inverted commas.
Note that a comma (within the inverted commas) marks the break between speech and narrative, and that another comma (after the narrative and before the second set of inverted commas) marks the resumption of the direct speech.
Note that the interrupted sentence of speech is resumed without the need for a capital letter.

◆ Longer speeches and the layout of dialogue.

> 'I should love to join you on Christmas Day,' said Sean.
> The children were ecstatic. They cried together,
> 'That's wonderful!'
> 'Indeed it is,' said my mother. 'When will you be able to get to us?'
> 'By 10 o'clock.'
> 'Really? That's splendid!'

→

The rule is 'a new line for a new speaker' even if the speech is only a word or two. In addition, each new speech should ideally be indented a little to make it easier for the reader to follow the cut and thrust of dialogue.
Note how a speech of two or more sentences is punctuated.

'Indeed it is,' said my mother. 'When will you be able to get to us?'

If this were lengthened further, the close of the second pair of inverted commas would be delayed accordingly:

'Indeed it is,' said my mother. 'When will you be able to get to us? Need I say "the earlier the better"? You know that we'll be up at the crack of dawn.'

◆ Inverted commas are used to enclose titles.

Have you read 'Angela's Ashes' by Frank McCourt?

Alternatively, the title can be underlined or, in print, italicised. Inverted commas will not then be needed.

◆ Inverted commas are used to enclose quotations.

Like Coriolanus, I often feel that 'there is a life elsewhere'.

Note that the final full stop comes outside the inverted commas enclosing the quotation. Incorporating a quotation in a sentence is different from punctuating direct speech.

See **INDIRECT/REPORTED SPEECH**.
See **TITLES**.

invisible
(*not* -able)

irational

Wrong spelling. See IRRATIONAL.

iridescent

(*not* -rr-)

irony or sarcasm?

IRONY is subtle, amusing, often witty.
SARCASM is deliberately hurtful and intentionally cruel.

Irony comes from a Greek word meaning 'pretended ignorance'. Sarcasm comes from a Greek word meaning 'to tear the flesh with one's teeth'.

Irony relies on those with insight realising that what is said is the opposite of what is meant.

Mr Bennet in Jane Austen's *Pride and Prejudice* frequently makes ironical remarks which only his more perceptive listeners will understand. When he tells one of his less musical daughters that she has delighted the company with her piano playing for long enough, she takes his remarks at face value. Jane and Elizabeth, two of her sisters, know exactly what he really meant.

Sarcasm sometimes uses this technique of irony and says in a very cutting way (which will be very clearly understood) the opposite of what is really meant.

When a teacher says, 'Brilliant!', to a pupil who fails yet again, he is being sarcastic and ironical at the same time. When a teacher says, 'Have you lost your tongue?' to a pupil, he is being sarcastic.

irrational

(*not* -r-)

irrelevant

(*not* irrevelant: think of 'does not relate')

irreparable

irreplaceable
See SOFT C AND SOFT G.

irrepressible

irresistible

irresponsible

irrevelant
Wrong spelling. See IRRELEVANT.

irreversible

irridescent
Wrong spelling. See IRIDESCENT.

-ise or -ize?
Most words ending with this suffix can be spelt -ise or -ize in British English. American English is more prescriptive and insists on -ize whenever there is a choice.

House-styles in Britain vary from publisher to publisher and from newspaper to newspaper. (You may have noticed that in this book I favour -ise.)

When making your choice, bear these two points in mind:

◆ These nineteen words *have* to be -ise: advertise, advise, apprise, arise, chastise, circumcise, comprise, compromise, despise, devise, disguise, enfranchise, excise, exercise, improvise, revise, supervise, surprise, televise.

◆ Only one verb of more than one syllable has to be -ize: capsize.
(One syllabled verbs like 'seize' still need care, of course.)

Whatever you decide, be consistent within one piece of writing and be consistent with derivatives. If you use 'realize' in one paragraph, you must use 'realization' and not 'realisation' at another point in the same piece. If you use 'sympathize', then you must refer to 'sympathizers' and not to 'sympathisers' elsewhere.

Many authorities prefer to use -ize when there is a choice. In practice, many writers prefer to use -ise because this choice is relatively trouble-free.

The decision is yours!

isn't

Place the apostrophe carefully. (*not* is'nt)

itinerary

(five syllables, not four as it is often mispronounced and misspelt)

its or it's?

ITS is a possessive adjective like 'her' and 'his':

The book has lost **ITS** cover.
ITS beauty has faded.

IT'S is a contraction of 'it is' or 'it has':

IT'S very cold today. (= it is)
IT'S been a long winter. (= it has)

If you are ever in doubt, see if you can expand 'its/it's' to 'it is' or 'it has'. If you can, you need an apostrophe. If you can't, you don't.

Remember too that contractions like 'it's' are fine in informal contexts but should be avoided in formal writing. When it's inappropriate to use slang, it is inappropriate to use these contractions. You have to write the forms in full.

J

jealous
(*not* jelous)

jealousy

jeopardise/jeopardize
Both spellings are correct.

jeopardy

jewelry/jewellery
Both spellings are correct.
(*not* jewlery as the word is often mispronounced)

jodhpurs

journey (singular) journeys (plural)
See PLURALS (iii).

judgement/judgment
Both spellings are correct.

judicial or judicious?
JUDICIAL = pertaining to courts of law and judges
JUDICIOUS = showing good judgment, wise,
prudent
The words are not interchangeable. There is a clear
distinction in meaning, as you can see.
A **JUDICIAL** decision is one reached in a law court.
A **JUDICIOUS** decision is a wise and discerning one.

K

keenness
keen + ness

kerb
See CURB OR KERB?.

kernel
See COLONEL OR KERNEL?.

kibbutz (singular) kibbutzim (plural)
See FOREIGN PLURALS.

kidnap
kidnapped, kidnapping, kidnapper
An exception to the 2-1-1 rule.
See ADDING ENDINGS (iv).

kneel
kneeled or knelt, kneeling

knew or new?
Use these exemplar sentences as a guide:

I **KNEW** the answer.
Nanette has **NEW** shoes.

knife (singular) knives (plural)
See PLURALS (v).

know or no?
Use these exemplar sentences as a guide:

I **KNOW** the answer.
NO, they cannot come.
We have **NO** milk left.

knowledge

knowledgeable/knowledgable
Both spellings are correct.

laboratory (singular) laboratories (plural)
See PLURALS (iii).

labour
laborious

laid
See ADDING ENDINGS (iii) (exception to rule).
See LAY OR LIE?.

lain
See LAY OR LIE?.

lama or llama?
LAMA = a Buddhist priest
LLAMA = an animal of the camel family

landscape
(*not* lanscape)

language
(*not* langage)

larva (singular) larvae (plural)
See FOREIGN PLURALS.

later or latter?
LATER is the comparative of 'late'.
(late, later, latest)

I will see you **LATER**.
You are **LATER** than I expected.

LATTER is the opposite of 'former'.
Cats and dogs are wonderful pets but the **LATTER**
need regular exercise.

Note: use 'latter' to indicate the second of two
references; use 'last' to indicate the final one of three
or more.

lay or lie?

The various tenses of these verbs cause a great deal of unnecessary confusion. Use these exemplar sentences as a guide:

to lay:
I **LAY** the table early every morning.
I **AM LAYING** the table now.
I **HAVE LAID** it already.
I **WAS LAYING** the table when you phoned.
I **LAID** the table before I went to bed.

My hen **LAYS** an egg every morning.
She **IS LAYING** an egg now.
She **HAS LAID** an egg already.
She **WAS LAYING** an egg when you phoned.
She **LAID** an egg every day last week.

to lie (down)
I **LIE** down every afternoon after lunch.
I **AM LYING** down now.
I **HAVE LAIN** down every afternoon this week.
I **WAS LYING** down when you phoned.
I **LAY** down yesterday afternoon.

to lie (= tell a lie)
I **LIE** regularly.
I **AM LYING** to you now.
I **HAVE LIED** all my life.
I **WAS LYING** to you last week.
I **LIED** to you yesterday as well.

laying

See LAY OR LIE?.

lead or led?

LEAD is the present tense.
LED is the past tense.

Go in front and **LEAD** us home.
He went in front and **LED** us home.

leaf (singular) leaves (plural)
> See PLURALS (v).

leaned/leant
> Both spellings are correct.

leaped/leapt
> Both spellings are correct.

learned/learnt
> Both spellings are correct.

leftenant
> Wrong spelling. See LIEUTENANT.

legend or myth?
> Both are traditional tales but legends usually have some basis in fact (e.g. Robert the Bruce and the spider, King Alfred and the cakes, Robin Hood and Sherwood Forest). Myths are supernatural tales, often involving gods or giants, which serve to explain natural events or phenomena (e.g. Pandora's Box and the coming of evil into the world, The Seven Pomegranate Seeds and the seasons of the year and so on).

legible
> See ELIGIBLE OR LEGIBLE?.

leisure
> (*not* -ie-)
> See EI/IE SPELLING RULE.

lend
> See BORROW OR LEND?.

less
> See FEWER OR LESS?.

liaise
> liaison (*not* liase/liason)

libel or slander?
Both refer to statements damaging to a person's character: **LIBEL** is written; **SLANDER** is spoken.

library
(*not* libary)

libretto (singular) libretti or librettos (plural)
See FOREIGN PLURALS.

licence or license?
LICENCE is a noun. We can refer to a licence or the licence or your licence:

Do you have your driving **LICENCE** with you?

LICENSE is a verb:

The restaurant is **LICENSED** for the consumption of alcohol.

licorice/liquorice
Both spellings are correct.

lie
See LAY OR LIE?.

lied
See LAY OR LIE?.

liesure
Wrong spelling. See LEISURE.

lieutenant

life (singular) lives (plural)
See PLURALS (v).

lighted/lit
Both forms are correct.

lightening or lightning?
LIGHTENING comes from the verb 'to lighten' and so you can talk about:

→

LIGHTENING a heavy load or **LIGHTENING** the colour of your hair.

LIGHTNING is the flash of light we get in the sky during a thunderstorm.

likable/likeable
Both spellings are correct.

like
> See AS OR LIKE?.

likelihood

liqueur or liquor?
> A **LIQUEUR** is a sweet, very strong, alcoholic drink usually taken in small glasses after a meal.
> **LIQUOR** refers to any alcoholic drink.

liquorice
> See LICORICE/LIQUORICE.

literally
> Beware of using 'literally' to support a fanciful comparison:

> ✗   My eyes **LITERALLY** popped out of my head when I saw her in a bikini. (They didn't!)
> ✓   My eyes popped out of my head when I saw her in a bikini.

> Everybody will understand that you are speaking figuratively (i.e. it was as if . . .).
> See METAPHOR.
> See SIMILE.

literati
> (*Not* litterari)
> This word is used to describe well-read and well-educated people who love literature.

literature
> (four syllables)

livelihood

loaf (singular) loaves (plural)
See PLURALS (v).

loath, loathe or loth?
LOATH and LOTH are interchangeable spellings and mean unwilling or reluctant:

I was **LOATH/LOTH** to hurt his feelings.

LOATHE means to detest:

I **LOATHE** snobbery.

loathsome
loathe + some = loathsome
This word means detestable.

loaves
See LOAF.

lonely
(*not* lonley)

loose or lose?
Use these exemplar sentences as a guide:

I have a **LOOSE** tooth. (rhymes with moose)
Don't **LOSE** your temper. (rhymes with snooze)

loping or lopping?
lope + ing = loping

He was **LOPING** along with long strides.

lop + ing = lopping

LOPPING the trees will just encourage them to grow taller.

See ADDING ENDINGS (i) and (ii).

a lot
(*never* alot)

→

Remember that this is a slang expression and should never be used in a formal context. Substitute 'many' or recast the sentence altogether.

lovable/loveable

Both spellings are correct.

luggage

(*not* lugage)

luxuriant or luxurious?

LUXURIANT = growing abundantly
LUXURIANT vegetation

LUXURIOUS = rich and costly, sumptuous
a **LUXURIOUS** hotel

luxury

-ly

Take care when adding this suffix to a word already ending in -l. You will have double -l:

real + ly   = really
ideal + ly   = ideally
special + ly = specially
usual + ly   = usually

lying

See LAY OR LIE?.

M

machinery
(*not* -ary)

madam or madame?
Use **MADAM**:

♦ as a polite term of respect:
Can I help you, madam?

♦ in letter writing:
Dear Madam (note capital letter)

♦ as a formal title of respect:
Thank you, Madam Speaker (note capital letter)

Use **MADAME** as the French equivalent:

♦ We are going to Madame Tussaud's.

♦ The famous French physicist, Madame Curie, was born in Poland.

magic -e
Also known as silent -e and mute -e.
See ADDING ENDINGS (ii).

mahogany

maintain

maintenance
(*not* maintainance)

manageable
See SOFT C AND SOFT G.

manager
(*not* manger, as is so often written!)

mango (singular) mangoes or mangos (plural)
See PLURALS (iv).

manoeuvre

mantelpiece
(*not* mantle-)

mantelshelf
(*not* mantle-)

margarine
(*not* margerine)

marihuana/marijuana
Both spellings are correct.

marriage

marvel
marvelled, marvelling

marvellous

masterful or masterly?
MASTERFUL = dominating
MASTERLY = very skilful

mathematics
(*not* mathmatics)

mating or matting?
mate + ing = mating
mat + ing = matting
See ADDING ENDINGS (i) + (ii).

matrix (singular) matrices or matrixes (plural)
See FOREIGN PLURALS.

may
See CAN OR MAY?.

may or might?
(i) Use may/might in a present context and might in a past context:
If I receive a written invitation, I **MAY/MIGHT** accept. (still possible)

If I had received a written invitation, I **MIGHT HAVE** accepted. (possibility over now)
If I don't hurry, I **MAY/MIGHT** miss the bus. (possibility exists)
If I hadn't hurried, I **MIGHT HAVE** missed the bus. (risk now over)

(ii) Convert 'may' to 'might' when changing direct speech to indirect or reported speech:

'**MAY** I come in?' she asked.
She asked if she **MIGHT** come in.
'You **MAY** be lucky,' she said.
She said that I **MIGHT** be lucky.

(iii) There is a slight difference between the meaning of 'may' and 'might' in the present tense when they are used in the sense of 'asking permission':
MAY I suggest that we adjourn the meeting? (agreement assured)
MIGHT I suggest that we adjourn the meeting? (suggestion more tentative)

me

See I/ME/MYSELF.

meant

(*not* ment, *not* mean't)

medal or meddle?

MEDAL = a small metal disc given as an honour
to **MEDDLE** = to interfere

mediaeval/medieval

Both spellings are correct.

medicine

(*not* medecine) medicinal

mediocre

Mediterranean

medium (singular) media or mediums (plural)
Note, however, that the two plurals differ in meaning.

The **MEDIA** hounded him to his death. (= radio, television, newspaper journalists)
She consulted a dozen **MEDIUMS** in the hope of making contact with her dead husband. (= people through whom the spirits of the dead are said to communicate)

mediums
See MEDIUM.

meet, meet up, meet up with, or meet with?
British English distinguishes between the first and last of these:
You **MEET** a person.
You **MEET WITH** an accident.
Avoid using 'meet up' and 'meet up with'. They are clumsy expressions.

✗   When shall we meet up?
✓   When shall we meet?

✗   We met up with friends in town.
✓   We met friends in town.

memento (singular) mementoes or mementos (plural)
See PLURALS (iv).

memorandum (singular) memoranda or memorandums (plural)
See FOREIGN PLURALS.

memory (singular) memories (plural)
See PLURALS (iii).

ment
Wrong spelling. See MEANT.

mention
mentioned, mentioning

Mesdames
(i) Plural of French *Madame.*
(ii) Used as a plural title before a number of ladies'
     names:

Mesdames Smith, Green, Brown and Kelly won
prizes.
Always used with an initial capital letter.

message

messenger
(*not* messanger)

metaphor
(*not* metaphore)
A metaphor is a compressed comparison:

He *wolfed* his food. (*note* the apparent identification
with a wolf's eating habits)

Compare SIMILE.

meteorology
(six syllables)

meter or metre?
Use these exemplar sentences as a guide:

Put these coins in the parking **METER**.
You'll need a **METRE** of material to make a skirt.
Sonnets are always written in iambic **METRE**.

might
See MAY OR MIGHT?.

might of
This is an incorrect construction.
See COULD OF.

milage/mileage
Both spellings are correct.

milieu (singular) milieus or milieux (plural)
See FOREIGN PLURALS.

militate or mitigate?
To **MILITATE** (against) comes from the Latin verb meaning 'to serve as a soldier' and it has the combative sense of having a powerful influence on something.

Despite his excellent qualifications, his youthful criminal record **MILITATED** against his appointment as school bursar.

To **MITIGATE** comes from the Latin adjective meaning 'mild' and it means to moderate, to make less severe.

Don't condemn the young man too harshly. There are **MITIGATING** circumstances.

millennium (singular) millennia or millenniums (plural) (*not* -n-)
See FOREIGN PLURALS.

millepede/millipede
Both spellings are correct.

mimic
mimicked, mimicking
See SOFT C AND SOFT G.

miniature

minuscule
(*not* miniscule)

minute
(*not* minuit)

miracle

miscellaneous
miscellany

mischief
> See EI/IE SPELLING RULE.

mischievous
> (*not* mischievious, as it is often mispronounced)

misplace
> See DISPLACE OR MISPLACE?.

misrelated participles
> See PARTICIPLES.

misspell
> mis + spell

misspelled/misspelt
> Both spellings are correct.

mistletoe

moccasin

modern
> (*not* modren)

moment
> (*not* momment)

momentary or momentous?
> **MOMENTARY** = lasting for only a very short time
> **MOMENTOUS** = of great significance

monastery (singular) monasteries (plural)
> (*not* monastry/monastries)
> See PLURALS (iii).

mongoose (singular) mongooses (plural)
> (*not* mongeese)

monotonous

moping or mopping?
> mope + ing = moping
> mop + ing = mopping
> See ADDING ENDINGS (i) + (ii).

moral or morale?
Use these exemplar sentences as a guide:

Denise is guided by strong **MORAL** principles.
My **MORALE** suffered badly when I failed my exams and I lost all faith in myself for years.

Morocco

mortgage
(*not* morgage as it is pronounced)

mosquito (singular) mosquitoes (plural)
See PLURALS (iv).

motto (singular) mottoes or mottos (plural)
See PLURALS (iv).

mould

mouldy

moustache

mucous or mucus?
MUCOUS is an adjective, as in **MUCOUS** membrane.
The name of the thick secretion of the mucous membrane is **MUCUS**.

murmur
murmured, murmuring (*not* murmer-)

mustn't
This is the contracted form of 'must not'.
Take care to place the apostrophe carefully.

must of
This is an incorrect construction.
See COULD OF.

mute -e
Also known as magic -e and silent -e.
See ADDING ENDINGS (ii).

mutual

reciprocal

Our dislike was **MUTUAL**.
Their marriage is based on **MUTUAL** respect.

Some would avoid the use of 'mutual' in expressions such as 'our mutual friend' because a third person is then introduced and the feelings of each person for the other two are not necessarily identical. It might be best here to describe the friend as one 'we have in common'.

myself

See I/ME/MYSELF.

myth

See LEGEND OR MYTH?.

N

naive/naïve
Both forms are correct.

naiveté/naïveté/naivety/naïvety
All these forms are correct.

nationalise or naturalise?
to **NATIONALISE** = to transfer ownership from the private sector to the state
to **NATURALISE** = to confer full citizenship on a foreigner

nebula (singular) nebulae or nebulas (plural)
See FOREIGN PLURALS.

necessary

necessity

negatives
See DOUBLE NEGATIVES.

neighbour
See EI/IE SPELLING RULE.

neither
See EI/IE SPELLING RULE.

neither...nor
Compare EITHER...OR.

nephew

-ness
Take care when adding this suffix to a word already ending in -n. You will have double n:

cleanness
openness
suddenness

neumonia

Wrong spelling. See PNEUMONIA.

new

See KNEW OR NEW?.

niece

See EI/IE SPELLING RULE.

nine

ninth

nineteen

nineteenth

ninety

ninetieth

no

See KNOW OR NO?.

no body or nobody?

Use these exemplar sentences as a guide:

It was believed that he had been murdered but **NO BODY** was ever found, and so nothing could be proved. (= no corpse)
NOBODY likes going to the dentist. (= no one)

none

The problem with 'none' is deciding whether to use with it a singular or a plural verb.

Strictly speaking, a singular verb should accompany 'none':

NONE of the passengers **WAS** hurt. (= not one)
NONE of the milk **WAS** spilt. (= not any)

Colloquially, a plural verb is often used when plural nouns follow the 'none of...' construction:

NONE of the passengers **WERE** hurt.
NONE of my friends **LIKE** pop music.

→

NONE of the children **WANT** an ice-cream.

Some reserve plural verbs in these cases for informal occasions; others would see them as perfectly acceptable formally as well.

no one
'No one' is singular and requires a singular verb:

NO ONE likes meanness.

'No one' should be written as two words and not hyphenated.

nosey/nosy
Both spellings are correct.
Note: for informal use only.

noticeable
(*not* noticable)
See SOFT C AND SOFT G.

not only ... but also
Take care with the positioning of each part of this pair:

✗   Denise not only enjoys composing but also conducting.

Denise enjoys two musical activities: composing, conducting.
   Put 'not only' in front of the first and 'but also' in front of the second, and let 'enjoys' refer to both.

✓   Denise enjoys **NOT ONLY** composing **BUT ALSO** conducting.

Compare BOTH...AND; EITHER...OR; NEITHER...NOR.

nouns
There are four kinds of nouns: common, proper, abstract and collective.

◆ Take care with the punctuation of *proper nouns*. Because they are the special individual names of people, towns, countries, newspapers, days of the week, businesses, and so on, they require initial capital letters:

Dennis Blakely
Ipswich
Sweden
The Times
Wednesday
Blazing Fireplaces Ltd.

Note that months of the year begin with a capital letter but the seasons generally do not:

April, the spring, but the Spring term.

◆ Do not confuse proper and *common nouns*.
labrador – common noun
Tinker – proper noun (needs initial capital)
    There is a certain flexibility in sentences like this:

Bishop Flynn will be arriving at three o'clock. The bishop/Bishop would like to meet the confirmation candidates before the service begins.

◆ *Abstract nouns* are the names of ideas, emotions, states of mind, and so on.
    The correct form can sometimes be difficult to remember. Do check in a dictionary when you are uncertain. Abstract nouns can have a huge variety of endings:

optimism, pride, complexity, failure, diffidence, depth, bravery, kindness, excitement, exhilaration, and so on.

Unsophisticated writers often add -ness to an adjective in the hope that it will then be

→

converted to an abstract noun. Sometimes this works; often it doesn't.

◆ *Collective nouns* (audience, flock, herd, congregation) are treated as singular nouns if regarded as a single whole:

The audience **WAS** wildly enthusiastic.

They are treated as plural nouns when regarded as a number of units making up the whole:

The jury **WERE** divided over his guilt.

nucleus (singular) nuclei (plural)
See FOREIGN PLURALS.

nuisance

number
See SINGULAR OR PLURAL?.

numbers
Should numbers be written in figures or in words? In mathematical, scientific, technical and business contexts, figures are used, as you would expect.

The problem arises in straightforward prose (an essay, perhaps, or a short story or a letter).

The rule of thumb is that small numbers are written as words and large numbers are written as figures.

What are small numbers? Some people would say numbers up to ten; others numbers up to twenty; others numbers up to one hundred. If you're not bound by the house-style of a particular organisation, you can make up your own mind. Numbers up to one hundred can be written in one or two words and this is why this particular cut-off point is favoured.

There were eight children at the party.
There were eighty-four/84 people in the audience.

Remember to hyphenate all compound numbers between twenty-one and ninety-nine when they are written as words.

Round numbers over one hundred, like two thousand, five million, and so on, are also usually written in words.

Write dates (21 October 2003) and sums of money (£10.50) and specific measurements (10.5 cm) in figures.

Time can be written in words or figures (three o'clock/3 o'clock) but 24-hour clock times are always written in figures (08.00).

Centuries can be written in words or figures (the 18th century/the eighteenth century).

It is important to be consistent within one piece of writing.

nursery (singular) nurseries (plural)
See PLURALS (iii).

O

oasis (singular) oases (plural)
See FOREIGN PLURALS.

obedience
(*not* -ance)

obedient
(not -ant)

occasion
occasional (*not* -ss-)

occasionally
occasional + ly

occur
occurred, occurring, occurrence
See ADDING ENDINGS (iv).

o'clock
Take care with the punctuation of this contraction.
The apostrophe represents the omission of four
letters:

o'clock = of the clock

Do *not* write: o'Clock, O'Clock or o,clock.

of or off?
These exemplar sentences may help:

He is the youngest **OF** four children. (pronounced *ov*)
Jump **OFF** the bus. (rhymes with cough)

Avoid the clumsy construction:

✗   Jump off of the bus.
✓   Jump off the bus.

official or officious?
OFFICIAL = authorised, formal

an **OFFICIAL** visit
an **OFFICIAL** invitation

OFFICIOUS = fussy, self-important, interfering

an **OFFICIOUS** secretary
an **OFFICIOUS** waiter

often

(*not* offen)

omission

omit

omitted, omitting
See ADDING ENDINGS (iv).

one

This can be a useful impersonal pronoun:

ONE never knows.

However, it can be difficult to keep up in a long
sentence:

ONE never knows if **ONE'S** husband is likely to
approve of **ONE'S** choice but that is a risk **ONE** has
to take.

Use 'one' sparingly and beware the risk of
pomposity.

only

The position of 'only' in a sentence is crucial to
meaning.
See AMBIGUITY (ii).

onnist

Wrong spelling. See HONEST.

onto or on to?

There are circumstances when the words must
always be written separately. We will consider these
first.

◆ Always write the words separately if 'to' is part of an infinitive (e.g. to eat, to speak, to be, to watch, etc.):

She drove **ON TO** test the brakes.

As a matter of interest you can double-check the 'separateness' of the two words by separating them further:

She drove **ON** because she wanted **TO** test the brakes.

◆ Always write the words separately when 'to' means 'towards':

We cycled **ON TO** Oxford.

Once again, the two words can be further separated:

We cycled **ON** the few remaining miles **TO** Oxford.

◆ It is permissible to write 'onto' or 'on to' when you mean 'to a position on':

The acrobat jumped **ONTO** the trapeze.
The acrobat jumped **ON TO** the trapeze.

It should be borne in mind, however, that many careful writers dislike 'onto' and always use 'on to'.

'Onto' is more common in American English but with the cautions expressed above.

ophthalmologist
(*not* opth-)

opinion
(*not* oppinion)

opposite

oral
See AURAL OR ORAL?.

organise/organize
Both spellings are correct.

original

originally
original + ly

ought
'Ought' is always followed by an infinitive (to visit, to read, to do, etc).

We **OUGHT** to write our thank-you letters.

The negative form is 'ought not'.

We **OUGHT NOT** to hand our work in late.

The forms 'didn't ought' and 'hadn't ought' are *always* wrong.

✗   He didn't ought to say this.
✓   He **OUGHT NOT** to say this.

✗   He hadn't ought to have hit her.
✓   He **OUGHT NOT** to have hit her.

ours
There are eight possessive pronouns:

mine, thine, his, hers, its, ours, yours, theirs. They never need an apostrophe:

This house is **OURS**.

outfit
outfitted, outfitting, outfitter
(exception to 2-1-1 rule).
See ADDING ENDINGS (iv).

out of
Avoid using 'of' unnecessarily:

✗   He threw it **OUT OF** the window.
✓   He threw it **OUT** the window.

outrageous

(*not* outragous)
See SOFT C AND SOFT G.

over-

Take care when adding this prefix to a word already beginning with r-. You will have -rr-:

overreact
overripe
overrule, etc.

overreact

over + react

ovum (singular) ova (plural)

See FOREIGN PLURALS.

owing to

See DUE TO/OWING TO.

packed

✗ We took a pack lunch with us.
✓ We took a **PACKED** lunch with us.

paid

(exception to the -y rule; *not* payed)
See ADDING ENDINGS (iii).

paiment

Wrong spelling. See PAYMENT.

pajamas

American spelling. See PYJAMAS.

palate, palette, pallet

PALATE = the top part of the inside of your mouth
PALETTE = a small board with a hole for the
thumb which an artist uses when mixing paints
PALLET = a platform used to lift and to carry
goods

panic

panicked, panicking, panicky
See SOFT C AND SOFT G.

paparazzo (singular) paparazzi (plural)

See FOREIGN PLURALS.

paraffin

paragraphing

There is no mystery about paragraphing although
many students find it difficult to know when to end
one paragraph and begin another.

A paragraph develops a particular point that is
relevant to the overall subject. If you wish to write a
letter or an essay that develops five or six points,
then each point will have its own paragraph and you
will add two more, one by way of an introductory   →

paragraph and another at the end as a conclusion.

There are no rules about how long a paragraph should be. Some paragraphs, often the introduction or the conclusion, may be a single sentence; other paragraphs may be a page or more long. Too many short paragraphs in succession can be very jerky; too many very long ones can look forbidding. It is best to mix long and short paragraphs, if you can.

You may also find that a paragraph which is becoming very long (a page or more) will benefit from being subdivided. The topic of the paragraph may be more sensibly developed as two or three subsidiary points.

Clear paragraphing is not possible without clear thinking. Think of what you want to say before you begin to write. List the topics or points you want to make in a sensible order. Then develop each one in turn in a separate paragraph.

A paragraph usually contains within it one sentence which sums up its topic. Sometimes the paragraph will begin with this sentence (called a topic sentence) and the rest of the paragraph will elaborate or illustrate the point made. Sometimes the topic sentence occurs during the paragraph. It can be effective, from time to time, to build up to the topic sentence as the last sentence in a paragraph.

Careful writers will try to move smoothly from one paragraph to the next, using link words or phrases such as: on the other hand; however; in conclusion.

In handwriting and in typing, it is usual to mark the beginning of a paragraph either by indenting it by 2cm or so, or by leaving a clear line between paragraphs. The only disadvantage of the latter method is that it is not always clear, when a sentence begins on a new page, whether a new paragraph is also intended.

Compare also the paragraphing of speech.
See INVERTED COMMAS.

paralyse/paralyze
Both spellings are correct.

paralysis

paraphernalia

parent
(*not* perant)

parenthesis (singular) parentheses (plural)
See FOREIGN PLURALS.

parliament

parliamentary

parrafin
Wrong spelling. See PARAFFIN.

partake or participate?
PARTAKE = to share with others (especially food and drink)
PARTICIPATE = to join in an activity; to play a part in

They **PARTOOK** solemnly of lamb, herbs and salt.
Will you be able to **PARTICIPATE** in the firm's pension scheme?

partener
Wrong spelling. See PARTNER.

participles
Participles help to complete some tenses.
Present participles end in -ing:

I am **COOKING**.
They were **WASHING**.
You would have been **CELEBRATING**.

→

Past participles generally end in -d or -ed but there are many exceptions:

I have **LABOURED**.
You are **AMAZED**.
It was **HEARD**.
We should have been **INFORMED**.

Care needs to be taken with the irregular forms of the past participle. They can be checked with a good dictionary.

to choose   chosen
to teach   taught
to begin   begun

The past participle is the word that completes the construction:

having been . . . .?

Participles can also be used as verbal adjectives (that is, as describing words with a lot of activity suggested):

a **HOWLING** baby
a **DESECRATED** grave

As verbal adjectives, they can begin sentences:

HOWLING loudly, the baby woke everyone up.
DESECRATED with graffiti, the tombstone was a sad sight.

Take care that the verbal adjective describes an appropriate noun or pronoun. A mismatch can result in unintended hilarity.
See AMBIGUITY (v).

particle

particular

particularly
particular + ly

partner
(*not* partener)

passed or past?
Use these exemplar sentences as a guide:

You **PASSED** me twice in town yesterday.
In the **PAST**, women had few rights.
In **PAST** times, women had few rights.
I walk **PAST** your house every day.

passenger
(*not* passanger)

past
See PASSED OR PAST?.

pastime
(*not* -tt-)

payed
Wrong spelling. See PAID.

payment
(*not* paiment)
See ADDING ENDINGS (iii).

peace or piece?
There were twenty-one years of **PEACE** between the two wars.
Would you like a **PIECE** of pie?

peculiar
(*not* perc-)

pedal or peddle?
a **PEDAL** = a lever you work with your foot
PEDDLE = to sell (especially drugs)

penicillin

peninsula or peninsular?

PENINSULA is a noun meaning a narrow piece of land jutting out from the mainland into the sea. It is derived from two Latin words: *paene* (almost) and *insula* (island).

Have you ever camped on the Lizard PENINSULA?

PENINSULAR is an adjective, derived from the noun:

The PENINSULAR War (1808–1814) was fought on the Iberian PENINSULA between the French and the British.

Note: It may be useful in a quiz to know that the P&O shipping line was in 1837 The Peninsular Steam Navigation Company (it operated between Britain and the Iberian Peninsula). In 1840, when its operation was extended to Egypt, it became the Peninsular and Oriental Steam Navigation Company (hence P&O).

people

(*not* peple)

perant

Wrong spelling. See PARENT.

per cent

(two words)

percentage

(one word)

perculiar

Wrong spelling. See PECULIAR.

perhaps

(*not* prehaps)

period

(*not* pieriod)

permanent
(*not* -ant)

permissible

perseverance
(*not* perser-)

personal or personnel?
Sarah has taken all her **PERSONAL** belongings with her.
She was upset by a barrage of **PERSONAL** remarks.
All the **PERSONNEL** will be trained in first aid.
Write to the **PERSONNEL** officer and see if a vacancy is coming up.

(*Note* the spelling of personnel with -nn-)
Note: Personnel Officers are now often called Human Resources Officers.

perspicacity or perspicuity?
PERSPICACITY = discernment, shrewdness, clearness of understanding
PERSPICUITY = lucidity, clearness of expression

phenomenon (singular) phenomena (plural)
See FOREIGN PLURALS.

physical

physically

physique

Piccadilly

piccalilli

picnic
picnicked, picnicking, picnicker
See SOFT C AND SOFT G.

piece

See PEACE OR PIECE?.

pieriod

Wrong spelling. See PERIOD.

pigmy/pygmy (singular) pigmies/pygmies (plural)

pining or pinning?

pine + ing = pining
pin + ing = pinning
See ADDING ENDINGS (i), (ii).

plateau (singular) plateaus or plateaux (plural)

See FOREIGN PLURALS.

plausible

pleasant

(*not* plesant)

pleasure

plural

See SINGULAR OR PLURAL?.

plurals

(i)   Most words form their plural by adding -s:

door doors; word words; bag bags; rainbow rainbows; shop shops; car cars

(ii) Words ending in a sibilant (a hissing sound) add -es to form their plural. This adds a syllable to their pronunciation and so you can always hear when this has happened:

bus buses; box boxes; fez fezes/fezzes; bench benches; bush bushes; hutch hutches.

(iii) Words ending in -y are a special case. Look at the letter that precedes the final -y. If the word ends in vowel + y, just add -s to form the plural (vowels: a, e, i, o, u):

day	days
donkey	donkeys
boy	boys
guy	guys

If the word ends in consonant + y, change the y to i, and add -es:

lobby	lobbies
opportunity	opportunities
body	bodies
century	centuries

This rule is well worth learning by heart. There are no exceptions. Remember an easy example as a key like boy/boys.

(iv) Words ending in -o generally add -s to form the plural:

piano	pianos
banjo	banjos
studio	studios
soprano	sopranos
photo	photos
kimono	kimonos

There are nine exceptions which add -es:

domino	dominoes
echo	echoes
embargo	embargoes
hero	heroes
mosquito	mosquitoes
no	noes
potato	potatoes
tomato	tomatoes
torpedo	torpedoes

About a dozen words can be either -s or -es and so you'll be safe with these. Interestingly, some of these words until recently have required -es →

(words like cargo, mango, memento, volcano). The trend is towards the regular -s ending and some words are in a transitional stage.

(v) Words ending in -f and -fe generally add -s to form the plural:

roof	roofs
cliff	cliffs
handkerchief	handkerchiefs
carafe	carafes
giraffe	giraffes

There are 13 exceptions which end in -ves in the plural. You can always hear when this is the case, but here is the complete list for reference:

knife/knives; life/lives; wife/wives; elf/elves; self/selves; shelf/shelves; calf/calves; half/halves; leaf/leaves; sheaf/sheaves; thief/thieves; loaf/loaves; wolf/wolves.

Four words can be either -fs or -ves:

hoofs/hooves; scarfs/scarves; turfs/turves; wharfs/wharves.

(vi) Some nouns are quite irregular in the formation of their plural.
Some words don't change:

aircraft, cannon, bison, cod, deer, sheep, trout

Some have a choice about changing or staying the same in the plural:

buffalo or buffaloes
Eskimo or Eskimos

Other everyday words have very peculiar plurals which perhaps we take for granted:

man	men	ox	oxen
woman	women	mouse	mice

child	children	louse	lice
foot	feet	die	dice
goose	geese		

After goose/geese, mongoose/mongooses seems very strange but is correct.

See also FOREIGN PLURALS.

pneumonia

possability
Wrong spelling. See POSSIBILITY.

possable
Wrong spelling. See POSSIBLE.

possess
possessed, possessing

possession

possessive apostrophes
See **APOSTROPHES** (ii), (iii).

possessive pronouns
No apostrophes are needed with possessive pronouns:

That is **MINE**.   That is **OURS**.
That is **THINE**.   That is **YOURS**.
That is **HERS**.   That is **THEIRS**.
That is **HIS**.
That is **ITS**.

possessor

possibility

possible
(*not* -able)

possible or probable?
POSSIBLE = could happen
PROBABLE = very likely to happen

potato (singular) potatoes (plural)
See PLURALS (iv).

practical or practicable?

A **PRACTICAL** person is one who is good at doing and making things.

A **PRACTICAL** suggestion is a sensible, realistic one that is likely to succeed.

A **PRACTICABLE** suggestion is merely one that will work. The word 'practicable' means 'able to be put into practice'. It does not carry all the additional meanings of 'practical'.

practice or practise?

Use these exemplar sentences as a guide:

PRACTICE makes perfect.
An hour's **PRACTICE** every day will yield returns.
The young doctor has built up a busy **PRACTICE**.

In the examples above, 'practice' is a noun.

You should **PRACTISE** every day.
PRACTISE now!

In these examples, 'practise' is a verb.

precede or proceed?

PRECEDE = to go in front of
PROCEED = to carry on, especially after having stopped

prefer

preferred, preferring, preference
See ADDING ENDINGS (iv).

prehaps

Wrong spelling. See PERHAPS.

prejudice

(*not* predjudice)

preparation

prepositions

Prepositions are small words like 'by', 'with', 'for', 'to', which are placed before nouns and pronouns to show how they connect with other words in the sentence:

They gave the flowers **TO** their mother.
Let him sit **NEAR** you.

Two problems can arise with prepositions.

(i) Take care to choose the correct preposition. A good dictionary will help you:

comply with
protest at
deficient in
ignorant of
similar to, and so on.

(ii) Don't take too seriously the oft-repeated advice not to end a sentence with a preposition. Use your discretion, and word your sentence however it sounds best to you.

Do you prefer the first or the second sentence here?

(a) **WITH** whom are you?
(b) Who are you **WITH**?

Which do you prefer here?

(c) She's a politician **FOR** whom I have a great deal of respect.
(d) She's a politician I have a great deal of respect **FOR**.

present

(*not* -ant)

presume
See ASSUME OR PRESUME?.

priest
See EI/IE SPELLING RULE.

primitive
(*not* -mat-)

principal or principle?
Use these exemplar sentences as a guide:

Rebuilding the school is their **PRINCIPAL** aim.
(= chief)
The **PRINCIPAL** announced the results. (= chief teacher)
His guiding **PRINCIPLE** was to judge no one hastily.
(= moral rule)

privilege
(*not* privelege or priviledge)

probable
See POSSIBLE OR PROBABLE?.

probably
(*not* propably)

procedure
(*not* proceedure)

proceed
See PRECEDE OR PROCEED?.

proclaim

proclamation
(*not* -claim-)

profession
(*not* -ff-)

professional

professor

profit
profited, profiting
See ADDING ENDINGS (iv).

prognosis
See DIAGNOSIS OR PROGNOSIS?.

prognosis (singular) prognoses (plural)
See FOREIGN PLURALS.

program or programme?
Use **PROGRAM** when referring to a computer
program.
Use **PROGRAMME** on all other occasions.

prominent
(*not* -ant)

pronounceable
(not pronouncable)
See SOFT C AND SOFT G.

pronouns
See I/ME/MYSELF.
See WHO/WHOM.
See POSSESSIVE PRONOUNS

pronunciation
(*not* pronounciation)

propably
Wrong spelling. See PROBABLY.

propaganda
(*not* propo-)

proper nouns
See NOUNS.

prophecy or prophesy?
These two words look very similar but are
pronounced differently.

→

The last syllable of **PROPHECY** rhymes with 'sea'; the last syllable of **PROPHESY** rhymes with 'sigh'.

Use the exemplar sentences as a guide:

Most of us believed her **PROPHECY** that the world would end on 31 December. (prophecy = a noun)

In the example above, you could substitute the noun 'prediction'.

We all heard him **PROPHESY** that the world would end at the weekend. (prophesy = a verb)

In the example above, you could substitute the verb 'predict'.

propoganda
Wrong spelling. See PROPAGANDA.

protein
See EI/IE SPELLING RULE.

psychiatrist

psychiatry

psychologist

psychology

publicly
(*not* publically)

punctuation
See under individual entries:
APOSTROPHES; BRACKETS; CAPITAL LETTERS; COLONS;
COMMAS; DASHES; EXCLAMATION MARKS; HYPHENS;
INVERTED COMMAS; SEMICOLONS; QUESTION MARKS.
See also END STOPS.

pyjamas
(American English: pajamas)

Q

quarrel
quarrelled, quarrelling
See ADDING ENDINGS (iv).

quarrelsome

quarter

question marks
A question mark is the correct end stop for a question. *Note* that it has its own built-in full stop and doesn't require another.

Has anyone seen my glasses?

Note that indirect questions do not require question marks because they have become statements in the process and need full stops.

He asked if anyone had seen his glasses.

See INDIRECT SPEECH/REPORTED SPEECH.

questionnaire
(*not* -n-)

questions (direct and indirect)
See QUESTION MARKS.
See INDIRECT SPEECH/REPORTED SPEECH.

queue
queued, queuing or queueing

quiet or quite?
The children were as **QUIET** as mice. (quiet = two syllables)
You are **QUITE** right. (quite = one syllable)

quotation or quote?
Use these exemplar sentences as a guide:

→

✓   Use as many **QUOTATIONS** as you can.

✗   Use as many quotes as you can. (quotation = a noun)

✓   I can **QUOTE** the whole poem. (quote = a verb)

quotation marks

See INVERTED COMMAS.

R

radiator
(*not* -er)

radically
radical + ly

radius (singular) radii or radiuses (plural)
See FOREIGN PLURALS.

raise or rise?
Let us look at these two words first as verbs (doing words):

My landlord has decided to **RAISE** the rent.
He **RAISED** the rent a year ago.
He has **RAISED** the rent three times in four years.
My expenses **RISE** all the time.
They **ROSE** very steeply last year.
They have **RISEN** steadily this year.

Now let us look at them as nouns (a raise, a rise):

✓ You should ask your employer for a **RISE**.
✗ You should ask your employer for a **RAISE**.

An increase in salary is called 'a rise' in the UK and 'a raise' in America.

raping or rapping?
rape + ing = raping
rap + ing = rapping
See ADDING ENDINGS (i), (ii).

rapt or wrapped?
RAPT = enraptured (**RAPT** in thought)
WRAPPED = enclosed in paper or soft material

raspberry
(*not* rasberry)

ratable/rateable
Both spellings are correct.

realise/realize
Both spellings are correct.

really
real + ly

reason

reasonable

rebut or refute?
REBUT = to take the opposite side in an argument
REFUTE = to prove an assertion or allegation to be wrong

reccomend
Wrong spelling. See RECOMMEND.

receipt
See EI/IE SPELLING RULE.

receive
See EI/IE SPELLING RULE.

recent or resent?
RECENT = happening not long ago
RESENT = to feel aggrieved and be indignant

recipe

recognise/recognize
Both spellings are correct.

recommend

recover or re-cover?
Bear in mind the difference in meaning that the hyphen makes:
RECOVER = get better, regain possession
RE-COVER = to cover again
See HYPHENS (iv).

rediculous
Wrong spelling. See RIDICULOUS.

refectory
(*not* refrectory)

refer
referred, referring, referee, reference
See ADDING ENDINGS (iv).

referee or umpire?
REFEREE = football, boxing
UMPIRE = baseball, cricket, tennis

refrigerator
(abbreviation = fridge)

refute
See REBUT OR REFUTE?

regal or royal?
REGAL = fit for a king or queen; resembling the behaviour of a king or queen
ROYAL = having the status of a king or queen, or being a member of their family

regret
regretted, regretting, regrettable, regretful
See ADDING ENDINGS (iv).

regretfully or regrettably?
REGRETFULLY = with regret
REGRETTABLY = unfortunately

rehearsal

rehearse

relevant
(*not* revelant)

relief
See EI/IE SPELLING RULE.

remember

(*not* rember)

repellent or repulsive?

Both words mean 'causing disgust or aversion'.
REPULSIVE, however, is the stronger of the two; it
has the sense of causing 'intense disgust', even
horror in some circumstances.
REPELLENT can also be used in the sense of being
able to repel particular pests (a mosquito repellent)
and in the sense of being impervious to certain
substances (water-repellent).

repetition

(*not* -pit-)

repetitious or repetitive?

Both words are derived from 'repetition'. Use
REPETITIOUS when you want to criticise
something spoken or written for containing tedious
and excessive repetition. 'Repetitious' is a derogatory
term.
Use **REPETITIVE** when you want to make the point
that speech, writing or an activity involves a certain
amount of repetition (e.g. work on an assembly line
in a factory). 'Repetitive' is a neutral word.

reported speech

See INDIRECT SPEECH/REPORTED SPEECH.

representative

repulsive

See REPELLENT OR REPULSIVE?.

resent

See RECENT OR RESENT?.

reservoir

From 'reserve'. (*not* resevoir)

resistance

reson
Wrong spelling. See REASON.

resonable
Wrong spelling. See REASONABLE.

responsibility
(*not* -ability)

responsible
(*not* -able)

restaurant

restaurateur
(*not* restauranteur)

resuscitate
(*not* rescusitate)

revelant
Wrong spelling. See RELEVANT.

revenge
See AVENGE OR REVENGE?.

reverend or reverent?
REVEREND = deserving reverence; title for a cleric

The Revd. C. Benson
The Rev. C. Benson

REVERENT = showing reverence
REVERENT pilgrims

reversible
(*not* -able)

rheumatism

rhubarb

rhyme

rhythm

ridiculous

(*not* rediculous)

The word comes from the Latin *ridere*, meaning 'to laugh'.

rigorous or vigorous?

RIGOROUS = exhaustive, very thorough, exacting physically or mentally

VIGOROUS = full of energy

robing or robbing?

robe + ing = robing

rob + ing = robbing

See ADDING ENDINGS (i) and (ii).

rococo

Romania/Rumania

Both spellings are correct.

A third variant, Roumania, is now considered old-fashioned and should be avoided.

roof (singular) roofs (plural) (*not* rooves)

royal

See REGAL OR ROYAL?.

S

sacrifice
(*not* sacra-)

sacrilege
(*not* sacra-)

safely
safe + ly

said
(exception to the -y rule)
See ADDING ENDINGS (iii).

salary

salmon

sanatorium (singular) sanatoria or sanatoriums (plural)
See FOREIGN PLURALS.

sandwich
(*not* sanwich)

sarcasm
See IRONY OR SARCASM?.

sat
See SIT.

satellite

Saturday

saucer

scan
Scan has a number of meanings in different subject
areas:

◆   It can mean to analyse the metre of a line of
    poetry.

→

♦ It can mean 'to look at all parts carefully in order to detect irregularities' (as in radar **SCANNING** and body **SCANNING**).

♦ It can mean to read intently and quickly in order to establish the relevant points.

When we talk of 'just **SCANNING** the headlines', we shouldn't mean 'glancing quickly over them without taking them in'. Scanning is a very intensive and selective process.

scarcely
This word needs care both in spelling and in usage. See DOUBLE NEGATIVES.

scarf (singular) scarfs or scarves (plural)
See PLURALS (v).

scaring or scarring?
scare + ing = scaring
scar + ing = scarring
See ADDING ENDINGS (i) and (ii).

scarsly
Wrong spelling. See SCARCELY.

scenery
(*not* -ary)

sceptic or septic?
A **SCEPTIC** is one who is inclined to doubt or question accepted truths.
SEPTIC is an adjective meaning 'infected by bacteria' (a **SEPTIC** wound).
It also describes the drainage system in country areas which uses bacteria to aid decomposition (**SEPTIC** drainage, a **SEPTIC** tank).

schedule

scheme

scissors

Scotch, Scots or Scottish?
Use **SCOTCH** only in such phrases as **SCOTCH** broth, **SCOTCH** whisky, **SCOTCH** eggs, **SCOTCH** mist and so on.

When referring to the people of Scotland, call them the **SCOTS** or the **SCOTTISH**. The term **SCOTCH** can cause offence.

The words **SCOTS** is often used in connection with aspects of language:

He has a strong **SCOTS** accent.
The **SCOTS** language is quite distinct from English.
What is the **SCOTS** word for 'small'?
We also talk about **SCOTS** law being different from English law.

In connection with people, we have the rather formal terms **Scotsman/Scotsmen** and **Scotswoman/Scotswomen**. Remember also the **Scots Guards**.

SCOTTISH is used rather more generally to refer to aspects of landscape and culture:

SCOTTISH history, **SCOTTISH** dancing, **SCOTTISH** traditions, **SCOTTISH** universities, the **SCOTTISH** Highlands

search

seasonable or seasonal?
SEASONABLE = normal for the time of year
(**SEASONABLE** weather)
SEASONAL = happening at a particular season
(**SEASONAL** employment)

secretary (singular) secretaries (plural) (*not* secer-)
See PLURALS (iii).

seize
> (*not* -ie-; an exception to the EI/IE SPELLING RULE)

self (singular) selves (plural)
> See PLURALS (v).

Sellophane
> Wrong spelling. See CELLOPHANE.

Sellotape
> (*not* cellotape)

semicolons
> Semicolons have two functions:

> (i) They can replace a full stop by joining two related sentences.

>> Ian is Scottish. His wife is Irish.
>> Ian is Scottish; his wife is Irish.

> (ii) They can replace the commas in a list which separate items. Semicolons are particularly useful with longer items where commas might be needed for other reasons.

>> Emily has bought some lovely things for her new flat: five huge, brightly coloured floor cushions; some woven throws, in neutral colours and of wonderful textures; an Afghan rug; a brilliant blue glass vase; and a wine-rack, very elegant, shaped like two Ss on their backs.

sensual or sensuous?
> **SENSUAL** = appealing to the body (especially through food, drink and sex)
> **SENSUOUS** = appealing to the senses aesthetically (especially through music, poetry, art)

sentence
> (*not* -ance)

sentiment or sentimentality?

SENTIMENT = a sincere emotional feeling
SENTIMENTALITY = over-indulgent, maudlin wallowing in emotion (sometimes with the suggestion of falseness and exaggeration)

sentimental

This adjective comes from both 'sentiment' and 'sentimentality' and so can be used in a fairly neutral way as well as a pejorative way:

SENTIMENTAL value (from sentiment)
for **SENTIMENTAL** reasons (from sentiment)
sickly **SENTIMENTAL** songs (from sentimentality)

separate

(*not* seperate)
Remember that there is A RAT in sep/A/RAT/e.

separate

separated, separating, separation
See ADDING ENDINGS (ii).

septic

See SCEPTIC OR SEPTIC?.

sequence of tenses

This means that tenses must match within a sentence. You have to keep within a certain time-zone:

✗ I telephoned everyone on the committee and tell them exactly what I thought.
✓ I telephoned everyone on the committee and **TOLD** them exactly what I thought.

✗ He said that he will ask her to marry him.
✓ He said that he **WOULD** ask her to marry him.

✗ I should be grateful if you will send me an application form.

→

✓ I should be grateful if you **WOULD** send me an application form.

✗ Fergal smiles at us, waves goodbye and was gone.

✓ Fergal smiles at us, waves goodbye and **IS** gone.

sergeant

(*not* sergant)

See SOFT C AND SOFT G.

serial

See CEREAL OR SERIAL?.

servere

Wrong spelling. See SEVERE.

serviceable

(*not* servicable)

See SOFT C AND SOFT G.

sesonable

Wrong spelling. See SEASONABLE OR SEASONAL?.

sesonal

Wrong spelling. See SEASONABLE OR SEASONAL?.

several

(three syllables)

severe

(*not* servere)

severely

severe + ly

sew or sow?

Use these exemplar sentences as a guide:

Sarah can **SEW** and knit beautifully.
She is **SEWING** her trousseau now.
She **SEWED** my daughter's christening gown by hand.
She has **SEWN** all her life.

The best time to **SOW** broad beans is in the autumn.
He's out now **SOWING** parsley and sage.
He **SOWED** seed that he saved from the year before.
He has **SOWN** the last of the lettuce seed.

sewage or sewerage?

SEWAGE = the waste products carried off by means of sewers

SEWERAGE = the provision of a drainage system

shall or will?

The simple future tense uses 'shall' with I and we and 'will' with the other pronouns:

I shall drive
you (singular) will drive
he/she/it will drive
we shall drive
you (plural) will drive
they will drive

By reversing 'shall' and 'will' you introduce a note of determination.

I will drive
you shall drive
he/she/it shall drive
we will drive
you shall drive
they shall drive

This distinction is lost in the contraction: I'll drive. However, in speech, the tone of voice will indicate which is intended.

shaming or shamming?

shame + ing = shaming
sham + ing = shamming
See **ADDING ENDINGS** (i) and (ii).

shan't

This contraction for 'shall not' would at one time have been punctuated with two apostrophes to indicate where letters have been omitted (sha'n't).

Use just one apostrophe nowadays (shan't).

See CONTRACTIONS.

sheaf (singular) sheaves (plural)

See PLURALS (v).

shear or sheer?

SHEAR is a verb (a doing word) and means to cut off.

SHEER is an adjective and means very thin (**SHEER** material), almost perpendicular (a **SHEER** cliff) or whole-hearted (**SHEER** delight).

sheikh

(also sheik, shaikh, shaykh – but these are less usual spellings)

shelf (singular) shelves (plural)

See PLURALS (v).

sheriff

(*not* -rr-)

shining or shinning?

shine + ing = shining

shin + ing = shinning

See ADDING ENDINGS (i) and (ii).

shoe

These are the tricky tenses of the verb 'to shoe':

The blacksmith **SHOES** the horse.

He is **SHOEING** the horse now.

He **SHOD** the horse last week.

He has **SHOD** the horse regularly.

should or would?

'Should' and 'would' follow the pattern of 'shall' and 'will'.

I should work
you (singular) would work
he/she/it would work
we should work
you (plural) would work
they would work

The correct construction often needed in a formal letter is:

I **SHOULD** be grateful if you **WOULD** send me . . .

In the sense of 'ought to', use 'should' in all cases:

I know I **SHOULD** apologise.
You **SHOULD** write to your parents.
She **SHOULD** understand if you explain.
He **SHOULD** understand.
We **SHOULD** repair the shed.
You all **SHOULD** work harder.
They **SHOULD** resign.

shouldn't
(*note* the position of the apostrophe)

should of
This is an incorrect construction.
See COULD OF.

shriek
(*not* shreik)
See EI/IE SPELLING RULE.

shy
shyer, shyest
Follows the -y rule.
See ADDING ENDINGS (iii).

shyly
(exception to the -y rule)
See ADDING ENDINGS (iii).

shyness
(exception to the -y rule)
See ADDING ENDINGS (iii).

siege
(*not* -ei)
See EI/IE SPELLING RULE.

sieve
See EI/IE SPELLING RULE.

sieze
Wrong spelling. See SEIZE.

sight
See CITE, SIGHT OR SITE?.

silent -e
Also known as magic -e and mute -e.
See ADDING ENDINGS (ii).

silhouette

silicon or silicone?
SILICON = element used in electronics industry
(**SILICON** chip)
SILICONE = compound containing silicon and used
in lubricants and polishes and in cosmetic surgery
(**SILICONE** implants)

similarly
similar + ly

simile
(*not* similie)
A simile is a comparison, usually beginning with
'like' or 'as'/'as if'.

You look *as if you've seen a ghost.*
Her hair was *like silk.*

Compare METAPHOR.

sincerely

sincere + ly (*not* sincerly)

Note the punctuation required when 'sincerely' is used as part of a complimentary close to a letter. Traditional layout:

> Yours sincerely,
> Aisling Hughes

Fully blocked layout:

Yours sincerely
Aisling Hughes

singeing or singing?

singe + ing = singeing
sing + ing = singing
See SOFT C AND SOFT G.

singular or plural?

(i) Always match singular subjects with singular verbs. Always match plural subjects with plural verbs.

The dog (singular) is barking (singular).
The dogs (plural) are barking (plural).

These pronouns are always singular:

everyone, everybody, everything
anyone, anybody, anything
someone, somebody, something
no one, nobody, nothing
either, neither, each

Everybody (singular) loves (singular) a sailor.

Remember that double subjects (compound subjects) are plural.

The Alsatian and the Pekinese (two dogs = plural subject) are barking (plural).

→

(ii) 'Either...or' and 'neither...nor' are followed by a singular verb.

Either James or Donal is lying and that's certain. (singular)

(iii) The choice between 'there is' (singular) and 'there are' (plural) will depend on what follows.

There is (singular) a good reason (singular) for his bad behaviour.

(iv) Take care to match nouns and pronouns.

    ✗ Ask any teacher (singular) and they (plural) will tell you what they (plural) think (plural) about the new curriculum.

    ✓ Ask any teacher (singular) and he or she (singular) will tell you what he or she (singular) thinks (singular) about the new curriculum.

(v) Don't be distracted by any additional details attached to the subject.

    ✗ The variety (singular) of courses available at the colleges were (plural) impressive.

    ✓ The variety (singular) of courses available at the colleges was (singular) impressive.

    ✓ The addition (singular) of so many responsibilities makes (singular) the job very stressful.

(vi) Collective nouns are singular when considered as a whole but plural when considered as combined units.

    ✗ The audience (singular) was divided (singular) in its (singular) response.

    ✓ The audience (here seen as a crowd of single people) were divided (plural) in their (plural) response.

sirocco/scirocco
Both spellings are correct.

sit
Don't confuse the grammatical formation of tenses:

We **SIT** by the fire in the evening and relax.
We **ARE SITTING** by the fire now.
We **ARE SEATED** by the fire.
We **HAVE BEEN SITTING** here all evening.
We **HAVE BEEN SEATED** here all evening.
We **SAT** by the fire yesterday.
We **WERE SITTING** by the fire when you phoned.
We **WERE SEATED** by the fire when you phoned.

Never write or say:

✗ We were sat.
Say ✓ We were sitting/we were seated.

site
See CITE, SIGHT OR SITE?.

siting or sitting?
site + ing = siting
sit + ing = sitting
See ADDING ENDINGS (i) and (ii).

sizable/sizeable
Both spellings are correct.

skein
See EI/IE SPELLING RULE.

skilful

skilfully
skilful + ly

slain
(exception to -y rule)
See ADDING ENDINGS (iii).

slander

See LIBEL OR SLANDER?.

slily/slyly

Both spellings are correct but the second is more commonly used.

sloping or slopping?

slope + ing = sloping
slop + ing = slopping

sly

slyer, slyest

slyly

See SLILY/SLYLY.

slyness

smelled/smelt

Both spellings are correct.

sniping or snipping?

snipe + ing = sniping
snip + ing = snipping

sobriquet/soubriquet

Both spellings are correct.

social or sociable?

SOCIAL = related to society
a **SOCIAL worker**, a **SOCIAL** problem, **SOCIAL** policy, **SOCIAL** housing

SOCIABLE = friendly

a very **SOCIABLE** person

These two words are quite distinct in meaning even though they may be used with the same noun:

a **SOCIAL** evening = an evening organised for the purpose of recreation
a **SOCIABLE** evening = a friendly evening where

everyone mixed well

With any luck the social evening was also a sociable one!

soft c and soft g

The letter c has two sounds. It can be hard and sound like k or it can be soft and sound like s.

The letter g has two sounds. It can be hard and sound like g in got and it can be soft and sound like j.

Usually, but not always, c and g sound hard when they precede a, o, u:

cat	cot	cut
gap	got	gut

They are generally soft when they precede e and i (and y):

cell	cider	cyberspace
germ	gin	gyrate

Sometimes an extra e is inserted into a word before a, o, u, so that the c or g in the word can sound soft:

noticeable   (*not* noticable)
manageable   (*not* managable)

Sometimes an extra k is inserted into a word between c and e, i, y, so that c can sound hard:

picnicker   (*not* picnicer)
trafficking   (*not* trafficing)

soldier

Take care with the spelling of this word.
(soldiers of the Queen, not soliders!)

soliloquy

somebody

(*not* sombody)

somersault

something
(*not* somthing)

some times or sometimes?
Use the exemplar sentences as a guide:

There are **SOME TIMES** when I want to leave
college. (= some occasions)
SOMETIMES I want to leave college. (= occasionally)

soubriquet
See SOBRIQUET/SOUBRIQUET.

souvenir

sovereign
(exception to the -ie- rule)
See EI/IE SPELLING RULE.

sow
See SEW OR SOW?.

spaghetti

speach
Wrong spelling. See SPEECH.

speak

specially
See ESPECIALLY OR SPECIALLY?.

speech
(*not* speach)

speech marks
See INVERTED COMMAS.

spelled/spelt
Both spellings are correct.

spilled/spilt
Both spellings are correct.

split infinitive

The infinitive of a verb is made up of two words:

to eat, to speak, to begin, to wonder

If a word (or a group of words) comes between the two words of an infinitive, the infinitive is said to be 'split'.

It is not a serious matter at all!

You may sometimes find it is effective to split an infinitive. Do so. On other occasions to split the infinitive may seem clumsy. Avoid doing so on those occasions. Use your own judgement.

Here are some examples of split infinitives:

to boldly go where no man has gone before
to categorically and emphatically deny any wrongdoing
to sometimes wonder how much will be achieved

They can easily be rewritten:

to go boldly
to deny categorically and emphatically
to wonder sometimes

spoiled/spoilt

Both spellings are correct.

stand

Don't confuse the grammatical formation of tenses.

We **STAND** by the window after breakfast.
We **ARE STANDING** now.
We **HAVE BEEN STANDING** for an hour.
We **STOOD** by the window yesterday.
We **WERE STANDING** there when you called.

Never write or say:

✗ We were stood.
Say ✓ We were standing.

stationary or stationery?
STATIONARY = standing still (a **STATIONARY** car)
STATIONERY = notepaper and envelopes

stiletto (singular) stilettos (plural)
See PLURALS (iv).

stimulant or stimulus?
Both words are related to 'stimulate' but there is a difference in meaning:
A **STIMULANT** is a temporary energiser like drink or drugs.
A **STIMULUS** is something that motivates (like competition).

stimulus (singular) stimuli (plural)
See FOREIGN PLURALS.

stomach ache

stood
See STAND.

storey (plural storeys) or story (plural stories)?
STOREY = one floor or level in a building

A bungalow is a single-**STOREY** structure.
A tower block can have twenty **STOREYS**.

STORY = a tale

I read a **STORY** each night to my little brother.
Children love **STORIES**.

strategem or strategy?
STRATEGEM = a plot, scheme, sometimes a trick, which will outwit an opponent or overcome a difficulty
STRATEGY = the overall plan for conducting a war or achieving a major objective

strategy or tactics?

STRATEGY = the overall plan or policy for achieving an objective
TACTICS = the procedures necessary to carry out the strategic policy

stratum (singular) strata (plural)
See FOREIGN PLURALS.

subjunctive

The subjunctive form of the verb is used to express possibilities, recommendations and wishes:

If he **WERE** a gentleman (and he's not) he would apologise on bended knee.
(✗ If he was a gentleman...)

If I **WERE** rich (and I'm not), I would help you.
(✗ If I was rich...)

I wish I **WERE** going with you (and sadly I'm not!).
(✗ I wish I was going with you.)

I recommend that he **BE** sacked immediately.
(✗ ... he is sacked)

I propose that the treasurer **LEAVE** the room.
(✗ .... leaves)

It is vital that these questions **BE** answered.
(✗ ... are answered)

The subjunctive is also used in these expressions but there is no change to the verb.

God **SAVE** the Queen.
God **BLESS** you.
Heaven **FORBID**.

submit

submitted, submitting
See ADDING ENDINGS (iv).

subtle

subtlety

subtly

success (singular) successes (plural)
See PLURALS (ii).

successful

successfully
successful + ly

sufferance

suffixes
See ADDING ENDINGS.

suggest
(*not* surjest)

superlative
See COMPARATIVE AND SUPERLATIVE.

supersede
(*not* -cede)

supervise
(*not* -ize)

surfeit
(*not* -ie-, exception to rule)
See EI/IE SPELLING RULE.

surjest
Wrong spelling. See SUGGEST.

surprise
(*not* suprise or surprize)

surprising

surreptitious

survivor

(*not* -er)

swam or swum?

Note these tenses of 'to swim':

I **SWAM** the Channel last year.
I have **SWUM** the Channel five times.

swinging or swingeing?

swing + ing = swinging
swinge + ing = swingeing
See SOFT C AND SOFT G.

swum

See SWAM OR SWUM?.

syllabus (singular) syllabuses or syllabi (plural)

See FOREIGN PLURALS.

synchronise/synchronize

Both spellings are correct.

synonym

synonymous

synopsis (singular) synopses (plural)

See FOREIGN PLURALS.

tableau (singular) tableaux (plural)
See FOREIGN PLURALS.

tactics
See STRATEGY OR TACTICS?.

taping or tapping?
tape + ing = taping
tap + ing = tapping

tariff
(*not* -rr-)

taught or taut?
Use these exemplar sentences as a guide:

Mrs Jenkins **TAUGHT** maths.
Hold the line **TAUT**. Pull it tight.

technical

tee shirt/T-shirt
Both versions are correct.

temperature
(four syllables)

tempo (singular) tempi or tempos (plural)
See FOREIGN PLURALS.

temporarily

temporary
(four syllables)

temprature
Wrong spelling. See TEMPERATURE.

tendency
(*not* -ancy)

tenses

See SEQUENCE OF TENSES.
See entries for individual verbs.

terminus (singular) termini or terminuses (plural)
See FOREIGN PLURALS.

terrible

(*not* -able)

testimonial or testimony?

TESTIMONIAL = formal statement in the
form of an open letter bearing witness to someone's
character, qualifications and relevant experience
TESTIMONY = formal written or spoken statement
of evidence, especially in a court of law

thank you or thank-you?

(never thankyou!)

I should like to **THANK YOU** very much for your
help.
THANK YOU for your help.
I have written all my **THANK-YOU** letters.

You will see that 'thank you' is NEVER written as one
word. It is hyphenated only when used as a compound
adjective describing 'letter' or another noun.

Those who care about such things can never bring
themselves to buy otherwise attractive thank-you cards
that have THANKYOU or THANK-YOU printed on
them!

their, there or they're?

Use these exemplar sentences as a guide:

They have sold **THEIR** house.
He is waiting for you over **THERE**.
THERE is no point in lying to me.
THEY'RE going to Krakow for Christmas. (= they
are)

theirs
(no apostrophe)

This is my dog; **THEIRS** has a white patch on his forehead.

theirselves
Incorrect formation. See THEMSELVES.

themselves
They blame **THEMSELVES** for the crash.
They **THEMSELVES** were there.

there
See THEIR, THERE OR THEY'RE?.

there is/there are
See SINGULAR OR PLURAL? (iii).

thesis (singular) theses (plural)
See FOREIGN PLURALS.

they're
See THEIR, THERE OR THEY'RE?.

thief (singular) thieves (plural)
See PLURALS (v).

thorough

thoroughly
thorough + ly

threshold
(*not* -hh-)

tingeing
See SOFT C AND SOFT G.

tiny
(*not* -ey)

tired
(*not* I am tiered)

I feel very **TIRED** today.

titbit

(*not* tidbit)

titles

When punctuating the title of a book, film, poem, song, etc., take care to begin the first word and all subsequent key words with a capital letter.

Have you read 'To Kill a Mockingbird' by Harper Lee?

Titles can be italicised (in print and word-processing) or underlined or enclosed in inverted commas (single or double).

The film *Schindler's List* is based on the book by Thomas Keneally called *Schindler's Ark*.
I'm so pleased that Diary of a Nobody is being serialised.
Have you seen the new production of 'Macbeth' at the Barbican?

to, too or two?

You should give this **TO** the police.
Do you know how **TO** swim?
(part of infinitive = to swim)
I was **TOO** embarrassed to say anything.
(= excessively)
Can we come **TOO**? (= also)
They have **TWO** houses, one in London and one in France.

tolerant

(*not* tollerant or tolerent)

tomato (singular) tomatoes (plural)

(an exception to rule)
See PLURALS (iv).

tomorrow
(*not* tommorrow)

tonsillitis

tornado (singular) tornadoes or tornados (plural)
See PLURALS (iv).

torpedo (singular) torpedoes (plural)
(an exception to rule)
See PLURALS (iv).

tortuous or torturous?
TORTUOUS = full of twists and turns, complex,
convoluted
TORTUROUS = painful, agonising, excruciating

total

totally
total + ly

toupee
(*not* toupée)

traffic
trafficked, trafficking, trafficker
See SOFT C AND SOFT G.

tragedy
(*not* tradgedy)

tragic
(*not* tradgic)

transfer
transferred, transferring, transference
See ADDING ENDINGS (iv).

transpire
Strictly speaking, this verb has two meanings:

◆ to give off moisture (of plant or leaf)
◆ to come slowly to be known, to leak out (of
secret information)

It is often used loosely in the sense of 'to happen'.
Why not use 'to happen' instead of this rather
pompous word?

travel

travelled, travelling, traveller
See ADDING ENDINGS (iv).

trivia

This is a plural noun and should be matched with a
plural verb.

Such **TRIVIA** are to be condemned.

troop or troupe?

TROOP refers to the armed forces or to groups of
people or particular animals:

a **TROOP** of scouts
a **TROOP** of children
a **TROOP** of monkeys

TROUPE refers to a group of touring actors,
dancers, musicians or other entertainers.

trooper or trouper?

TROOPER = cavalry soldier or member of an
armoured unit

He swears like a **TROOPER** at nine years old.

TROUPER = a touring entertainer

Jack Densley is a grand old **TROUPER**.

truly

(*not* truely, an exception to the -y rule)
See ADDING ENDINGS (ii).

try

tried, trying
See ADDING ENDINGS (iii).

tumulus (singular) tumuli (plural)
See FOREIGN PLURALS.

turf (singular) turfs or turves (plural)
See PLURALS (v).

twelfth
(*not* twelth, as it is often mispronounced)

twentieth
See ADDING ENDINGS (iii).

twenty

typical

typically
typical + ly

ultimatum (singular) ultimata or ultimatums (plural)
See FOREIGN PLURALS.

umbrella
(*not* umberella)

umpire
See REFEREE OR UMPIRE?.

un-
Remember that when un- is added to a word
beginning with n-, you will have
-nn-:

un + natural = unnatural
un + nerve   = unnerve

unconscious

under-
Remember that when you add under- to a word
beginning with r-, you will have -rr-:

under + rate = underrate

underlay or underlie?
Use these exemplar sentences as a guide:

to **UNDERLAY** = to lay or place under
You should **UNDERLAY** the carpet with felt if your
floorboards are very uneven.
I **UNDERLAID** this carpet with very thick felt
because the floorboards were so uneven.
This carpet **IS UNDERLAID** with felt.

to **UNDERLIE** = to be situated under (esp. rocks)

Granite **UNDERLIES** the sandstone here.
Granite **UNDERLAY** the sandstone, as we soon
discovered.

→

The sandstone here **IS UNDERLAIN** by granite.

also:

The **UNDERLYING** problem is poverty.

Compare LAY OR LIE?.

underrate
under + rate

undoubtedly

unequivocally
unequivocal + ly (*not* unequivocably)

unexceptionable or unexceptional?
UNEXCEPTIONABLE = inoffensive, not likely to
cause criticism or objections
UNEXCEPTIONAL = ordinary, run-of-the-mill

Compare EXCEPTIONABLE OR EXCEPTIONAL?.

unget-at-able
(*not* un-get-at-able)

uninterested
See DISINTERESTED OR UNINTERESTED?.

unique
Remember, that 'unique' is absolute. It means 'the
only one of its kind'. Something is either unique or
it's not. It can't be 'quite unique' or 'very unique'.

unmanageable
(*not* unmanagable)
See SOFT C AND SOFT G.

unmistakable/unmistakeable
Both spellings are correct.

unnatural
un + natural

unnecessary
un + necessary

unparalleled

until
(*not* untill)

unusually
unusual + ly

upon
(*not* apon)

upstairs
(one word)

urban or urbane?
URBAN = relating to a town or city
URBAN population
URBANE = suave, courteous

used to
✓ I **USED TO** like him very much

The negative form is:

✓ I **USED NOT TO** like him very much.
✗ I didn't used to like him.

useful

useless

usurper
(*not* -or)

vase

vechicle
Wrong spelling. See VEHICLE.

vegetable
(*not* vegtable)

vegetation

vehicle
(*not* vechicle)

veil
See EI/IE SPELLING RULE.

venal or venial?
VENAL = open to bribery and corruption
VENIAL = minor, excusable, pardonable

vengeance
(*not* vengance)
See SOFT C AND SOFT G.

ventilation
(*not* venta-)

veracity or voracity?
VERACITY = truthfulness
VORACITY = greed

veranda/verandah
Both spellings are correct.

vertebra (singular) vertebrae (plural)
See FOREIGN PLURALS.

veterinary
(five syllables!)

vice versa

vicious

view

vigorous
(*not* vigourous)
See also RIGOROUS OR VIGOROUS?.

vigour

villain

violent

virtuoso (singular) virtuosi or virtuosos (plural)
See FOREIGN PLURALS.

visible
(*not* -able)

visitor
(*not* -er)

vocabulary
(five syllables)

volcano (singular) volcanoes or volcanos (plural)
See PLURALS (iv).

voluntary

volunteer
volunteered, volunteering

voracity
See VERACITY OR VORACITY?.

vortex (singular) vortexes or vortices (plural)
See FOREIGN PLURALS.

vowels
Five letters of the alphabet are always vowels:

a e i o u

→

The letter y is sometimes a vowel and sometimes a consonant.

Y is a vowel when it sounds like e or i:

pretty, busy
sly, pylon

Y is a consonant at the beginning of syllables and words and has a different sound:

yellow, beyond

W

waist or waste?
Use these exemplar sentences as a guide:

Tie this rope around your **WAIST**.
Don't **WASTE** paper.
What do you do with **WASTE** paper?
Industrial **WASTE** causes pollution.

waive or wave?
WAIVE = to give something up or not exact it

I shall **WAIVE** the fine on this occasion.

WAVE = to move something to and fro

WAVE to the Queen.

wander or wonder?
I love to **WANDER** through the forest.
(rhymes with girl's name, Wanda)
I **WONDER** what has happened to him.
(rhymes with 'under')

wasn't
Place the apostrophe carefully.

waste
See WAIST OR WASTE?.

wave
See WAIVE OR WAVE?.

weak or week?
WEAK = feeble
WEEK = seven days

weather or whether?
Use these exemplar sentences as a guide:

The **WEATHER** this winter has been awful.
I don't know **WHETHER** I can help. (= if)

Wednesday
(*not* Wensday)

week
See WEAK OR WEEK?.

weir
(exception to the -ie- rule)
See EI/IE SPELLING RULE.

weird
(exception to the -ie- rule)
See EI/IE SPELLING RULE.

Wensday
Wrong spelling. See WEDNESDAY.

were or where?
Use these exemplar sentences as a guide:

We **WERE** walking very fast. (rhymes with 'her')
WHERE are you? (rhymes with 'air')
Do you know **WHERE** he is?
This is the house **WHERE** I was born.

weren't
Place the apostrophe carefully.

wharf (singular) wharfs or wharves (plural)

where
See WERE OR WHERE?.

whether
See WEATHER OR WHETHER?.

whilst
(exception to magic -e rule)
See ADDING ENDINGS (ii).

whiskey or whisky?
WHISKEY is distilled in Ireland.
WHISKY is distilled in Scotland.

who or whom?

The grammatical distinction is that 'who' is a subject pronoun and 'whom' is an object pronoun.

(i) Use this method to double-check whether you need a subject pronoun or an object pronoun when who/whom begins a question:

Ask yourself the question and anticipate the answer. If this could be one of the subject pronouns (I, he, she, we or they), then you need 'who' at the beginning of the question:

Who/whom is there?
The answer could be: *I* am there.
✓ **WHO** is there?

If the answer could be one of the object pronouns (me, him, her, us or them), then you need 'whom' at the beginning of the question:

Who/whom did you meet when you went to London?
The answer could be: I met *him*.
✓ **WHOM** did you meet?

(ii) Use this method if who/whom comes in the middle of a sentence:

Break the sentence into two sentences and see whether a subject pronoun (I, he, she, we, they) is needed in the second sentence or an object pronoun (me, him, her, us, them).

Here is the man who/whom can help you.

Divide into two sentences:

Here is the man. *He* can help you.
✓ Here is the man **WHO** can help you.

He is a writer who/whom I have admired for years.

→

Divide into two sentences:

He is a writer. I have admired *him* for years.

✓ He is a writer **WHOM** I have admired for years.

whole

See HOLE OR WHOLE?.

wholly

(exception to the magic e- rule)
See ADDING ENDINGS (ii).

who's or whose?

Use these exemplar sentences as a guide:

WHO'S been eating my porridge? (= who has)
WHO'S coming to supper? (= who is)
WHOSE calculator is this? (= belonging to whom)
There's a girl **WHOSE** cat was killed.

wierd

Wrong spelling. See WEIRD.

wife (singular) wives (plural)

See PLURALS (v).

wilful

(*not* willful)

will

See SHALL OR WILL?.

wining or winning?

wine + ing = wining
win + ing = winning
See ADDING ENDINGS (i) and (ii).

wisdom

(exception to magic -e rule)
See ADDING ENDINGS (ii).

withhold

(*not* withold)

wolf (singular) wolves (plural)
See PLURALS (v).

woman (singular) women (plural)
See PLURALS (vi).

wonder
See WANDER OR WONDER?.

won't
See CONTRACTIONS.

woollen
(*not* woolen)

worship
worshipped, worshipping, worshipper
(exception to 2-1-1 rule)
See ADDING ENDINGS (iv).

would
See SHOULD OR WOULD?.

wouldn't
Take care to place the apostrophe correctly.

would of
Incorrect construction.
See COULD OF.

wrapped
See RAPT OR WRAPPED?.

wreath or wreathe?
Use these exemplar sentences as a guide:

She lay a **WREATH** of lilies on his grave. (= noun)
Look at him **WREATHED** in cigarette smoke. (verb, rhymes with 'seethed')

write
Use these sentences as a guide to tenses:

I **WRITE** to her every day.

→

I **AM WRITING** a letter now.
I **WROTE** yesterday.
I have **WRITTEN** every day.

writer

(*not* writter)

wry

wrier or wryer, wriest or wryest

wryly

(exception to the y- rule)
See ADDING ENDINGS (iii).

wryness

(exception to the -y rule)
See ADDING ENDINGS (iii).

Y

-y rule

See ADDINGS ENDINGS (iii).
See PLURALS (iii).

yacht

yield

See EI/IE SPELLING RULE.

yoghurt/youghourt/yougurt

All these spellings are correct.

yoke or yolk?

Use these exemplar sentences as a guide:

The **YOKE** of the christening gown was beautifully embroidered.
The oxen were **YOKED** together.
She will eat only the **YOLK** of the egg.

your or you're?

Use these exemplar sentences as a guide:

YOUR essay is excellent. (= belonging to you)
YOU'RE joking! (= you are)

yours

This is **YOURS**.
No apostrophe needed!

Z

zealot

zealous

zealously

Zimmer frame

zloty (singular) zloties or zlotys (plural)
   See PLURALS (iii).

zoological

zoology

APPENDIX A Literary terms

Here are a few of the most widely used literary devices. You will probably be familiar with them in practice but perhaps cannot always put a name to them.

alliteration   the repetition of sounds at the beginning of words and syllables
- Around the rugged rocks the ragged rascals ran.

climax   ◆ I came; I saw; I conquered!

epigram   a short pithy saying
- Truth is never pure, and rarely simple. (Oscar Wilde)

euphemism   an indirect way of referring to distressing or unpalatable facts
- I've *lost* both my parents. (= they've died)
- She's rather *light-fingered*. (= she's a thief)

hyperbole   exaggeration
- Jack cut his knee rather badly and lost *gallons* of blood.
- What's for lunch? I'm *starving*.
- I loved Ophelia. *Forty thousand brothers Could not, with all their quantity of love, Make up my sum.* (Shakespeare: 'Hamlet')

irony   saying one thing while clearly meaning the opposite
- For Brutus is an *honourable* man. (Shakespeare: 'Julius Caesar')

litotes   understatement
- He was *not exactly polite*. (= very rude)
- I am a citizen of *no mean city*. (= St Paul boasting about Tarsus and hence about himself)

metaphor   a compressed comparison

- Anna *flew* downstairs. (i.e. her speed resembled the speed of a bird in flight)
- Sleep that *knits up the ravelled sleeve of care.* (Shakespeare: 'Macbeth')
- No man is *an island, entire of itself.* (John Donne)

metonymy   the substitution of something closely associated
- The *bottle* has been his downfall. (= alcohol)
- The *kettle's* boiling. (= the water in the kettle)
- The *pen* is mightier than the *sword.* (= what is written)

onomatopoeia   echoing the sound
- Bees *buzz*; sausages *sizzle* in the pan; ice-cubes *tinkle* in the glass.

Frequently, alliteration, vowel sounds and selected consonants come together to evoke the sounds being described:

- Only the monstrous anger of the guns
  Only the stuttering rifles' rapid rattle
  Can patter out their hasty orisons.
    (Wilfred Owen: 'Anthem for Doomed Youth')

oxymoron   apparently contradictory terms which make sense at a deeper level
- The *cruel mercy* of the executioner brought him peace at last.

paradox   a deliberately contradictory statement on the surface which challenges you to discover the underlying truth
- If a thing is worth doing, it's worth doing badly. (G. K. Chesterton)

personification   describing abstract concepts and inanimate objects as though they were people
- Death *lays his icy hand* on kings. (James Shirley)

Often human feelings are also attributed. This extension of personification is called the **pathetic fallacy**.

◆ The wind *sobbed* and *shrieked in impotent rage*.

pun a play on words by calling upon two meanings at once

◆ Is life worth living? It depends on the *liver*.

rhetorical question no answer needed!

◆ Do you *want* to fail your exam?

simile a comparison introduced by 'like', 'as', 'as if' or 'as though'

◆ O, my Luve's *like a red red rose*
That's newly sprung in June. (Robert Burns)

◆ I wandered lonely *as a cloud*. (William Wordsworth)

◆ You look *as if you've seen a ghost*.

synecdoche referring to the whole when only a part is meant, or vice versa

◆ *England* has lost the Davis Cup. (= one person)

◆ *All hands* on deck!

transferred epithet moving the adjective from the person it describes to an object

◆ She sent an *apologetic* letter.

◆ He tossed all night on a *sleepless* pillow.

zeugma grammatical play on two applications of a word

◆ She *swallowed* her pride and three dry sherries.

◆ She went straight home *in* a flood of tears and a sedan chair. (Charles Dickens: 'The Pickwick Papers')

Each part of speech has a separate function.

Verbs are 'being' and 'doing' words.
It *seems*.
She *is laughing*.
All the pupils *have tried* hard.
Note also these three verb forms: the infinitive (*to seem*); the present participle (*trying*); the past participle (*spoken*).
Adverbs mainly describe verbs.
He spoke *masterfully*. (= how)
She *often* cries. (= when)
My grandparents live *here*. (= where)
Nouns are names (of objects, people, places, emotions, collections, and so on).
common noun: *table*
proper noun: *Emma*
abstract noun: *friendship*
collective noun: *swarm*
Pronouns take the place of nouns.
He loves me. *This* is *mine*. *Who* cares? *I* do.
Adjectives describe nouns and pronouns.
a *hard* exercise   a *noisy* class   *red* wine
Conjunctions are joining words.
co-ordinating: fish *and* chips; naughty *but* nice;
now *or* never
subordinating: We trusted him *because* he was
honest.
She'll accept *if* you ask her.
Everyone knows *that* you are doing
your best.
Prepositions show how nouns and pronouns relate to the rest of the sentence.
Put it *in* the box. Phone me *on* Thursday. Give it *to* me. Wait *by* the war memorial. She's the boss *of* Tesco.

Interjections are short exclamations.
Hi! Ouch! Hurray! Ugh! Oh! Shh! Hear, hear!
The articles: definite (*the*)
indefinite (*a*; *an* – singular; *some* – plural)

Planning

Whenever you have an important essay, letter, report or article to write, it's well worth taking time to work out in advance exactly what you want to say. Consider also the response you hope to get from those who read the finished document and decide on the tone and style which would be most appropriate.

- Next, jot down, as they come into your head, all the points that you want to include. Don't try to sort them into any order. Brainstorm. (It's better to have too much material at this stage than too little.)
- Then, read through these jottings critically, rejecting any that no longer seem relevant or helpful.
- Group related points together. These will form the basis of future paragraphs.
- Sequence these groups of points into a logical and persuasive order.
- Decide on an effective introduction and conclusion.

Drafting

Now you are ready to write the first draft.

- Concentrate on conveying clearly all that you want to say, guided by the structure of your plan.
- Choose your words with care. Aim at the right level of formality or informality.
- Put to one side any doubts about spelling, punctuation, grammar or usage. These can be checked later. (If you wish, you can pencil

queries in the margin, or key in a run of question marks – ?????.)

◆ When you have finished this first draft, read it critically, concentrating initially on content. (It can help to read aloud.) Have you included everything? Is your meaning always clear? Should some points be expanded? Should some be omitted? Have you repeated yourself unnecessarily?

◆ Read the amended text again, this time checking that you have maintained the appropriate tone. Make any adjustments that may be needed.

◆ Examine the paragraphing. Does each paragraph deal adequately with each topic? Should any paragraphs be expanded? Should any be divided? Should the order be changed? Does each paragraph link easily with the next? Are you happy with the opening and closing paragraphs? (Sometimes they work better when they are reversed.) Should any paragraphs be jettisoned?

◆ Are you happy with the layout and the presentation?

◆ If you have made a lot of alterations, you may wish to make a neat copy at this stage. Read through again, critically, making any adjustments that you feel necessary. You may find third and fourth drafts are needed if you are working on a really important document. Don't begrudge the time and effort. Much may depend on the outcome.

Proofreading

When you are happy with the content, style and tone, you are ready to proofread. Proofreading means scrutinising the text for spelling, punctuation, grammar, usage and typographical errors.

- Make yourself read very slowly. Best of all, read aloud. Read sentence by sentence, paragraph by paragraph. Read what is actually there, not what you *meant* to write.
- Check anything that seems doubtful. Check all the queries you tentatively raised earlier. Don't skimp this vital penultimate stage. Don't rely wholly on a computer spellcheck; it will take you only so far (and, in some cases, introduce errors of its own).
- If you know you have a particular weakness (spelling, perhaps, or not marking sentence boundaries – commas are not substitutes for full stops!), then devote one read-through exclusively to this special area.
- When you are satisfied that you have made this important document as good as you possibly can, you are ready to make the final neat version. If, in the process, you make any small errors, don't simply cross them out and don't use correction fluid. Rewrite. When the last word is written, you can be satisfied that you have done your very best. Good luck!

Note: If you have a form to fill in, it is well worth making a few photocopies before you start. Practise what you want to say on the photocopies. Fit what you want to say carefully in the space available. Then complete the original form. It's well worth the extra time taken.